THE
NEW YORKER
BOOK OF NEW YORK CARTOONS

PRINCETON

Bloomberg PRESS

EDITED BY ROBERT MANKOFF

THE
NEW YORKER
BOOK OF NEW YORK CARTOONS

PUBLISHED BY BLOOMBERG PRESS

To purchase framed prints of cartoons or to license cartoons for use in periodicals, Web sites, or other media, please contact CARTOONBANK.COM, a New Yorker Magazine company, at 145 Palisade Street, Suite 373, Dobbs Ferry, NY 10522, Tel: 800-897-TOON, or (914) 478-5527, Fax: (914) 478-5604, e-mail: toon@cartoonbank.com, Web: www.cartoonbank.com.

Books are available for bulk purchases at special discounts. Special editions or book excerpts can also be created to specifications. For information, please write: Special Markets Department, Bloomberg Press.

First edition published 2004
1 3 5 7 9 10 8 6 4 2

Library of Congress Cataloging-in-Publication Data

The New Yorker book of New York cartoons / edited by Robert Mankoff.
    p. cm.
    Includes index.
    ISBN 1-57660-128-5 (alk. paper)
     1. New York (N.Y.)--Caricatures and cartoons. 2. American wit and humor, Pictorial. 3. New Yorker (New York, N.Y. : 1925) I. Title: Book of New York cartoons. II. Mankoff, Robert. III. New Yorker (New York, N.Y. : 1925)

NC1428.N47 2004
741.5'973--dc22   2004043693

Book design by LAURIE LOHNE / Design It Communications

THE
NEW YORKER
BOOK OF NEW YORK CARTOONS

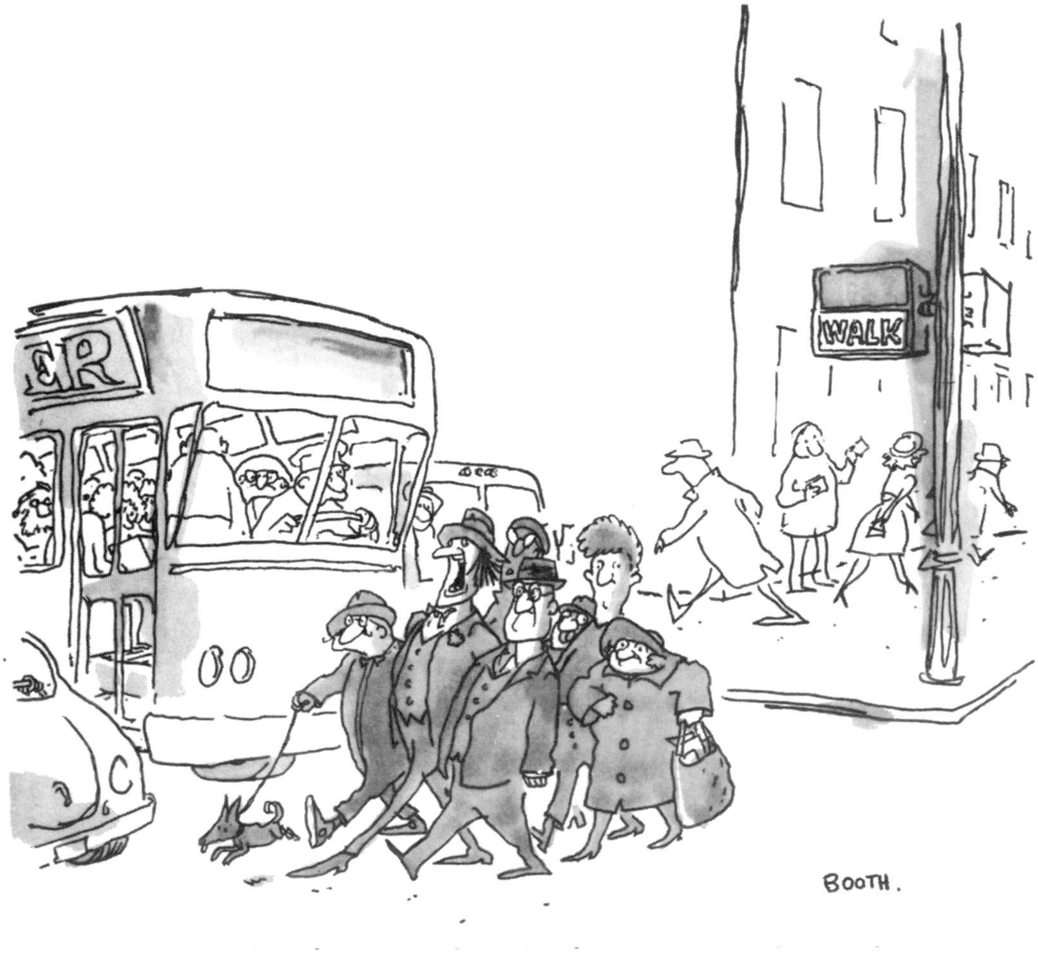
ER
WALK
BOOTH.

"My mother always says that. She always says 'You have to be a little bit crazy to live in New York.' Mother is a little crazy, but she doesn't live in New York. She lives in Nishnabotna, Missouri."

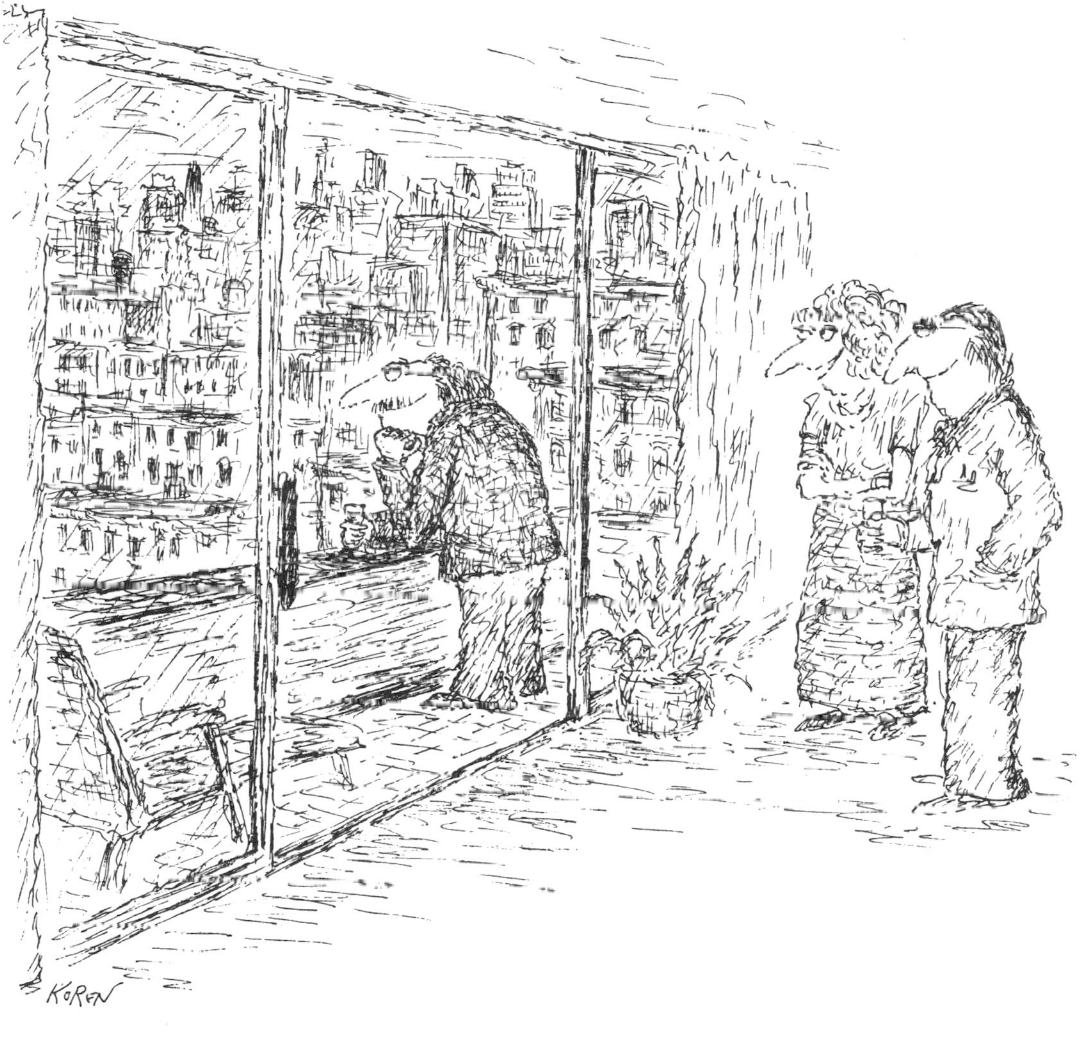
KOREN

"New York is a constant nourishment for Daniel."

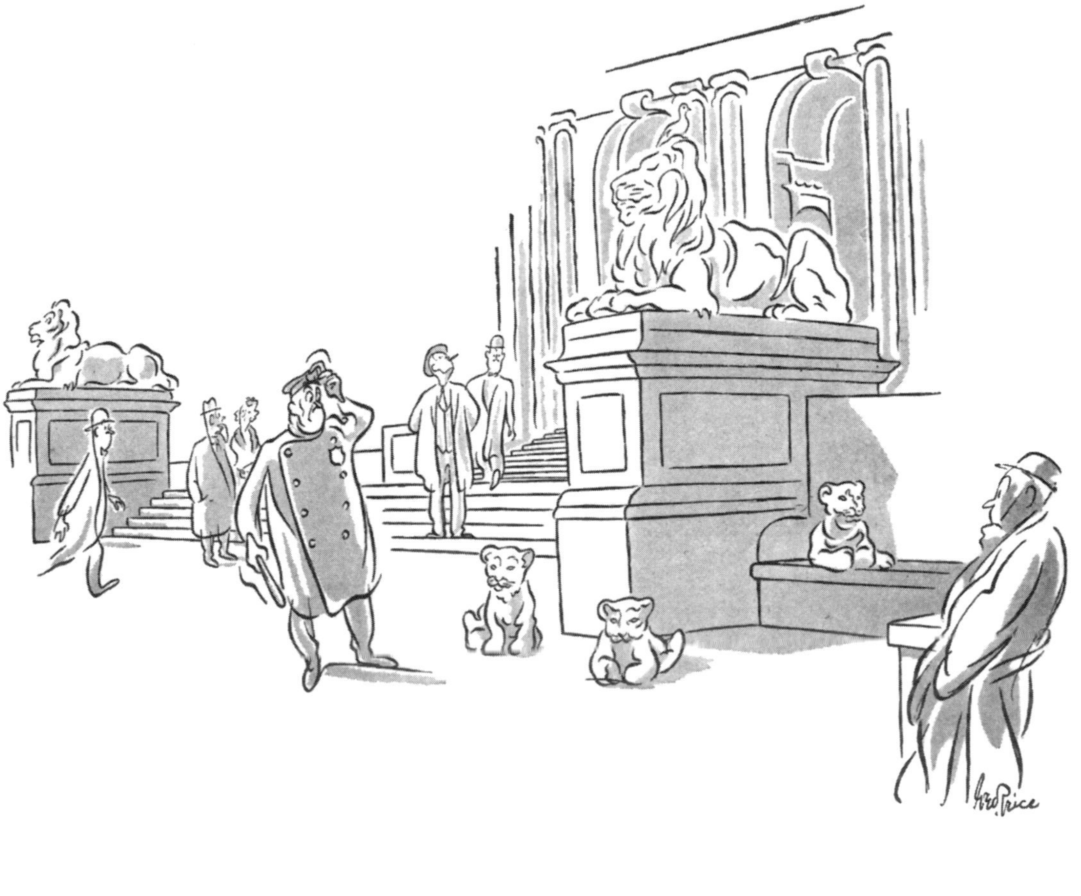
Geo. Price

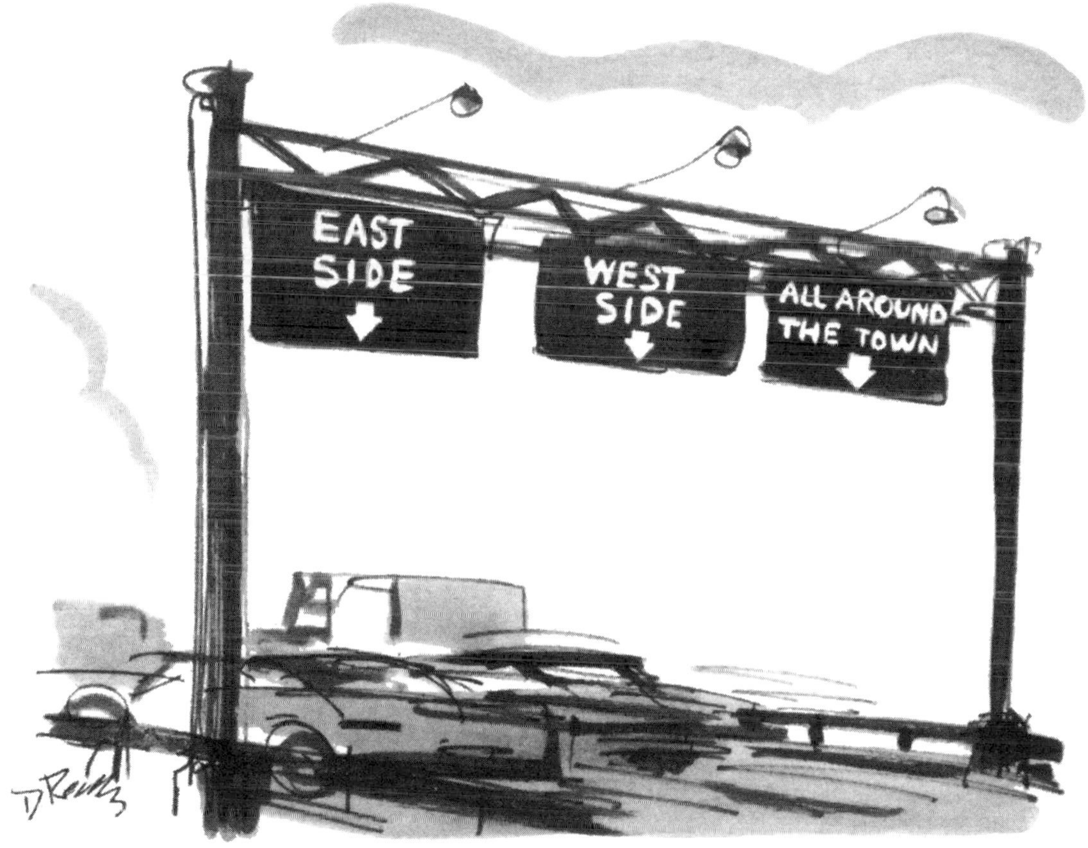
EAST SIDE
WEST SIDE
ALL AROUND THE TOWN

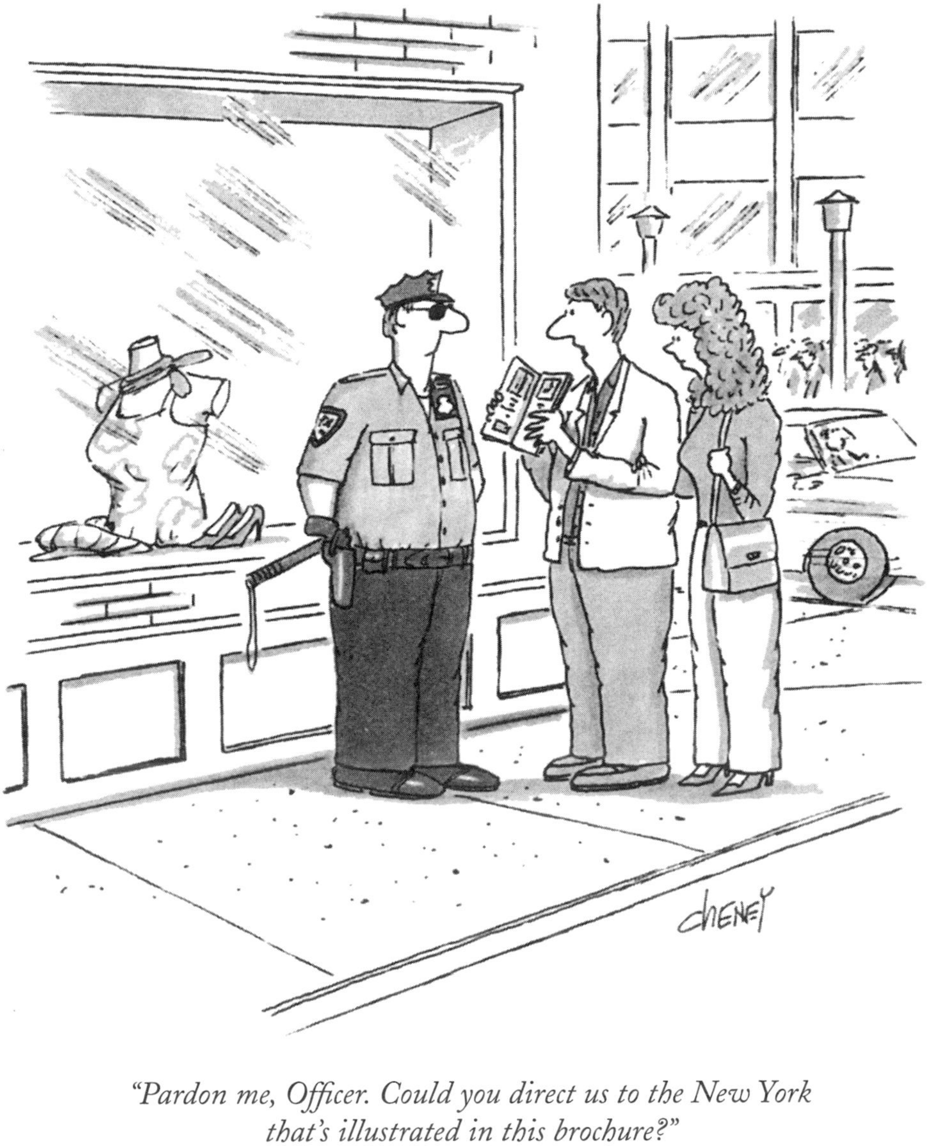

cheney

"Pardon me, Officer. Could you direct us to the New York that's illustrated in this brochure?"

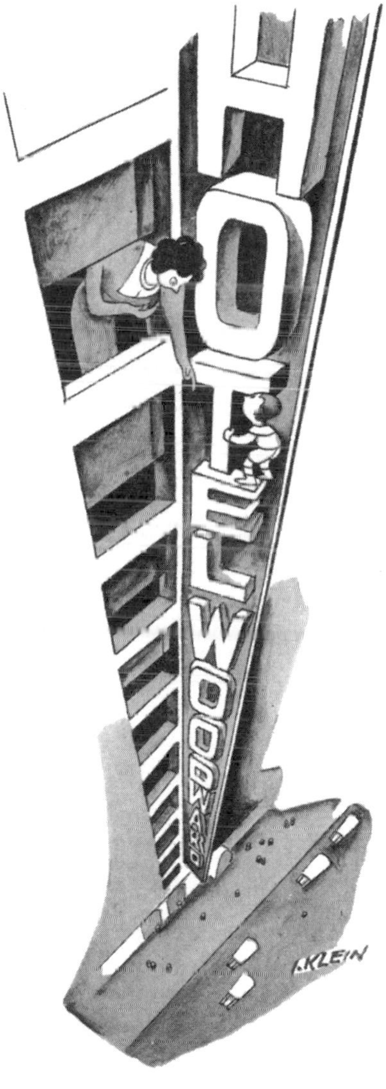
HOTEL WOODWARD
I. KLEIN

"... and don't go beyond W, Harold!"

NO PARKING 9 DAYS OUT OF 10

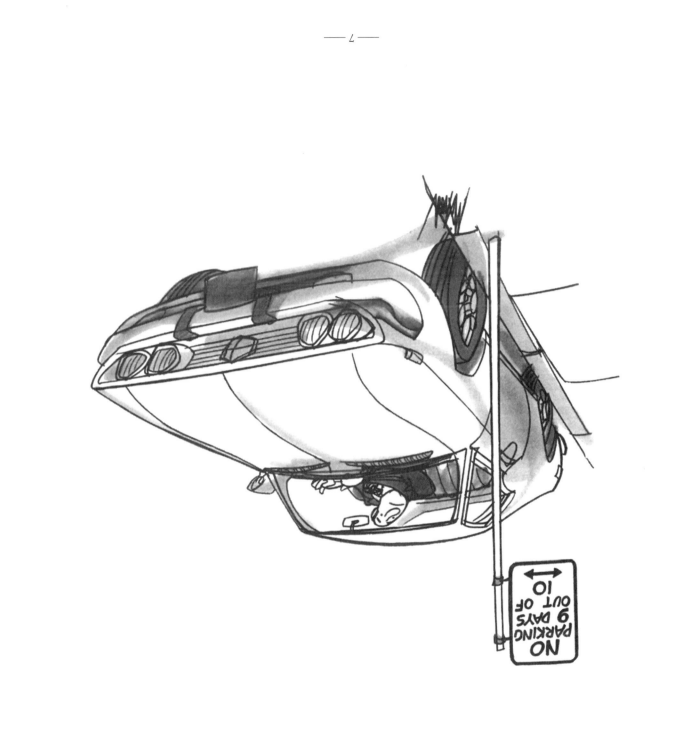

NEW YORK THERAPY CLOCK
YOU HAVE BEEN IN THERAPY FOR:
18 YEARS 14 DAYS 45 MINUTES
Victoria Roberts

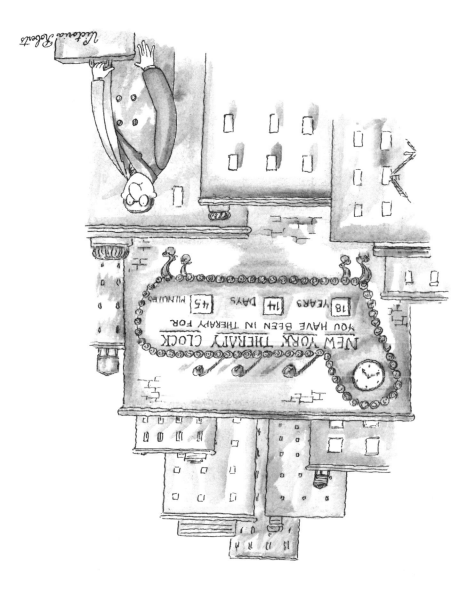

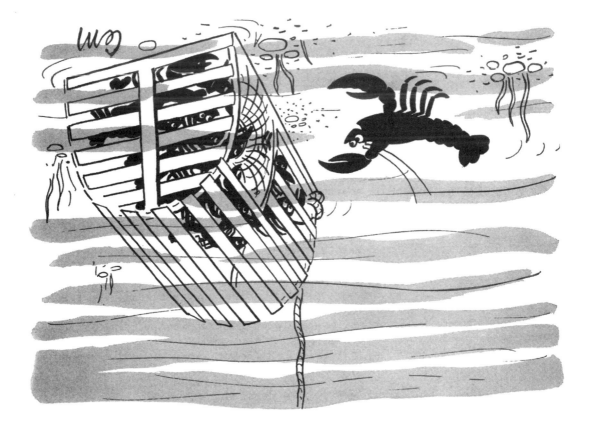

"Give my regards to Broadway."

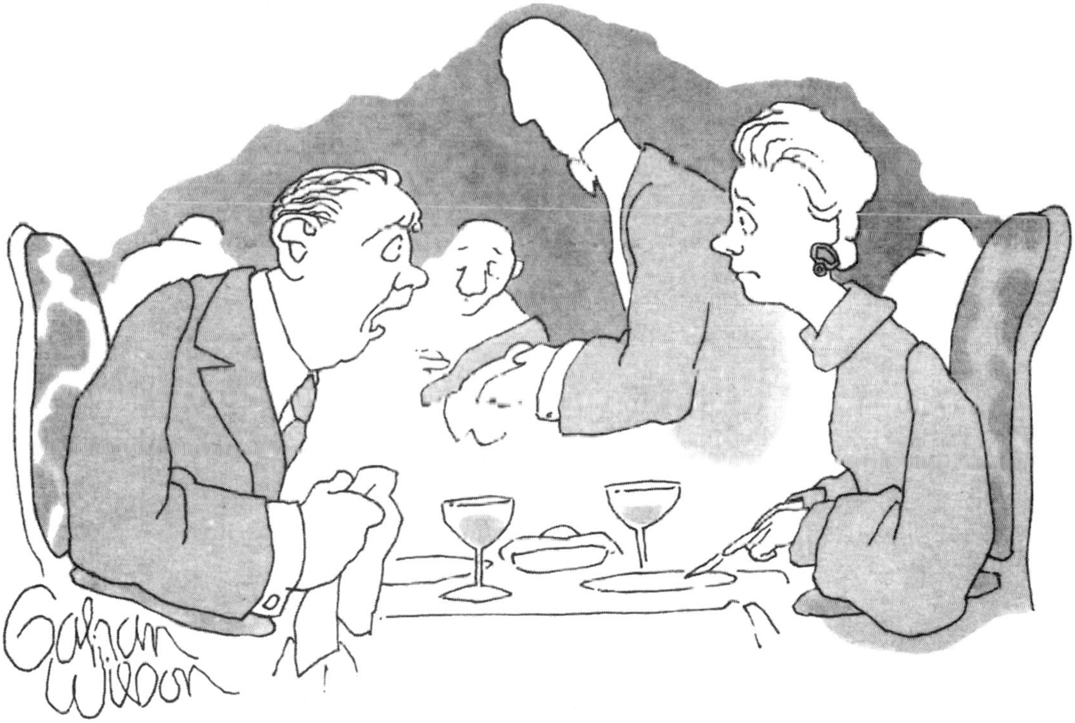
Gahan Wilson

"Sometimes I have this awful feeling I'm really a West Side person."

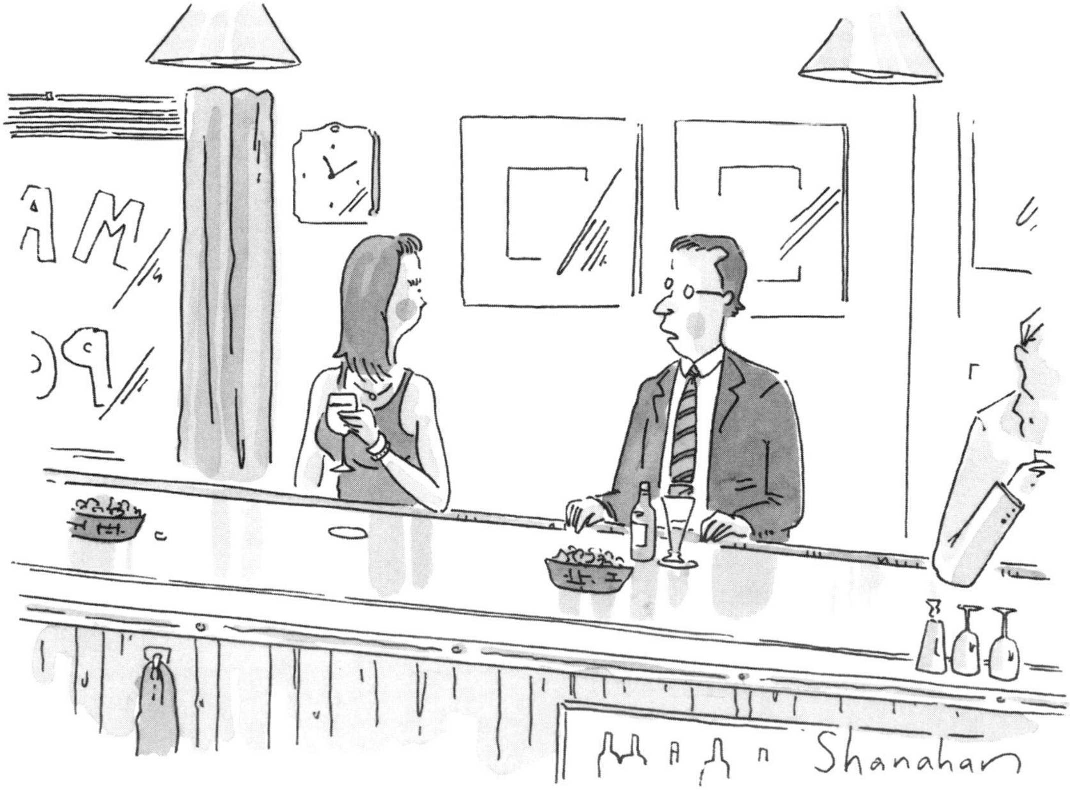
Shanahan

"Would you like to go to my place for a cigarette?"

"It's so lovely out here you wonder why they
have it so far from the city."

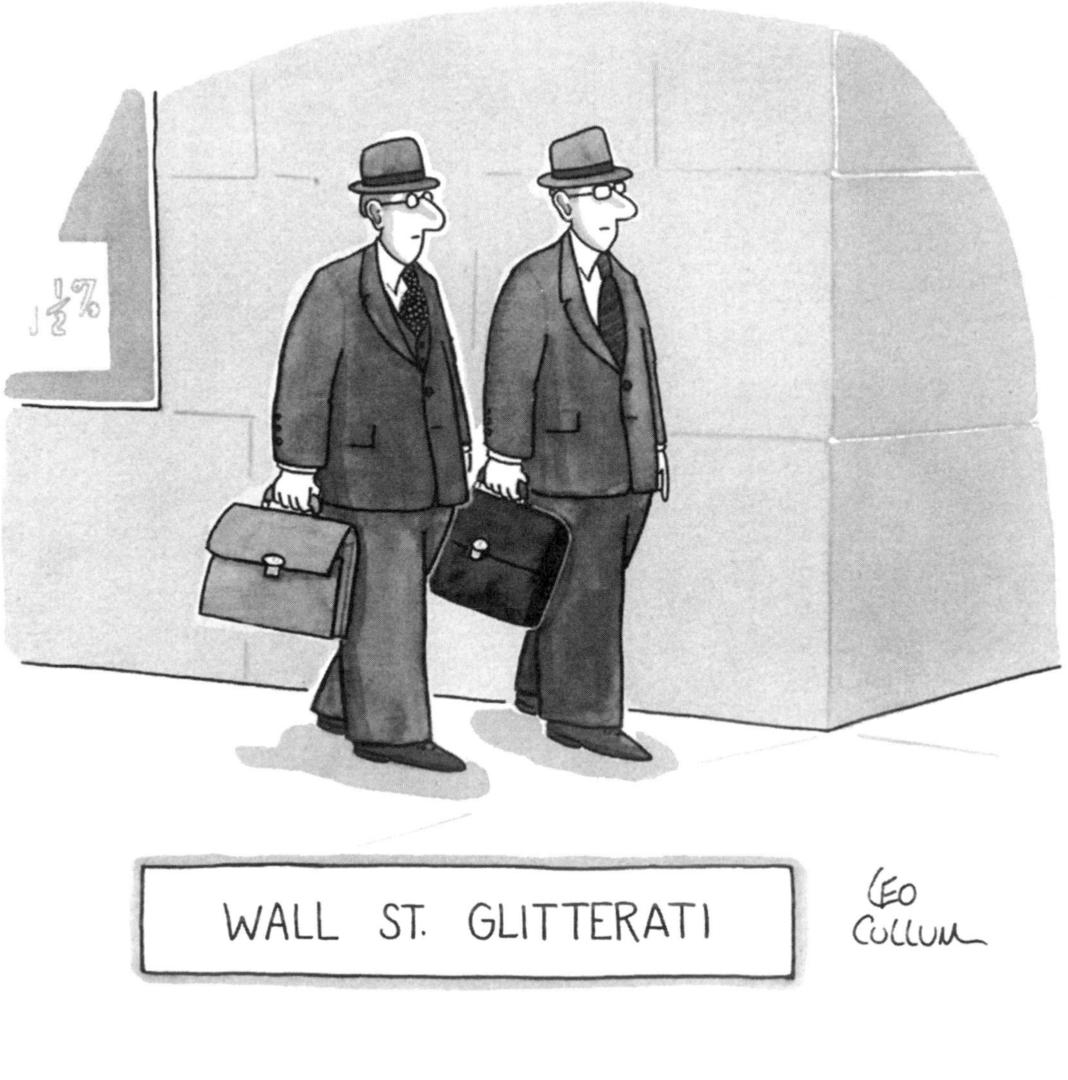
1½%
WALL ST. GLITTERATI
LEO CULLUM

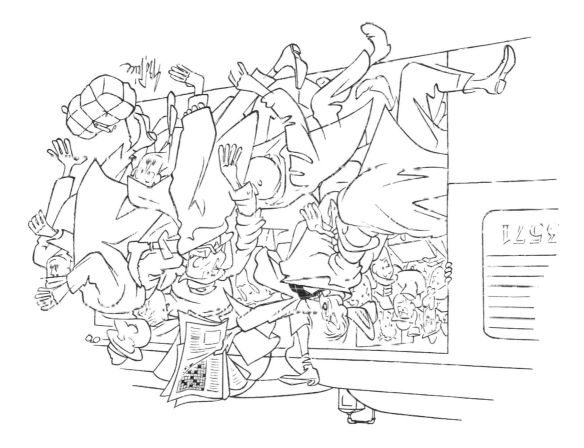

"Somebody did my crossword puzzle!"

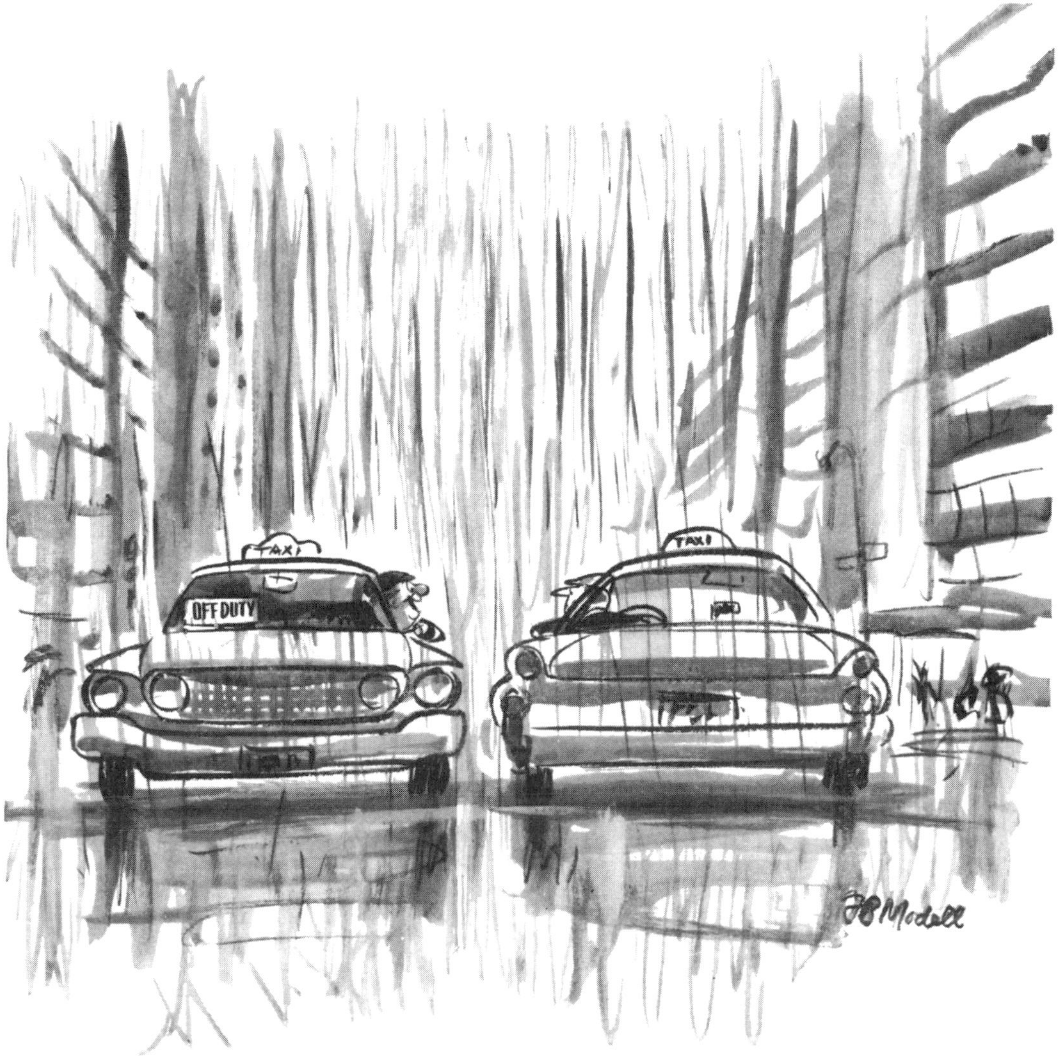
TAXI
OFF DUTY
TAXI
JB Modell

"Actually, I'm not off duty. I'm just having some fun."

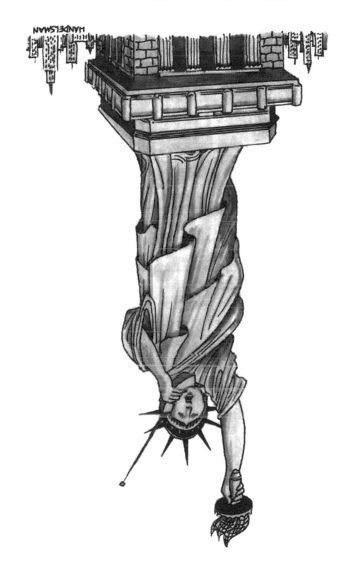

"Well, it all depends. Where are these
huddled masses coming from?"

ENTERING THE UPPER EAST SIDE
VISITORS MUST SIGN IN
MStevens

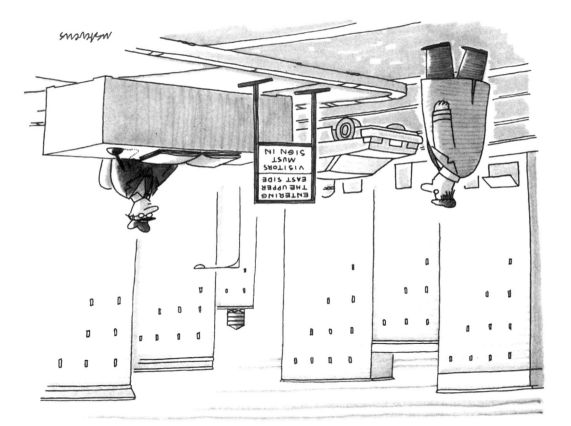

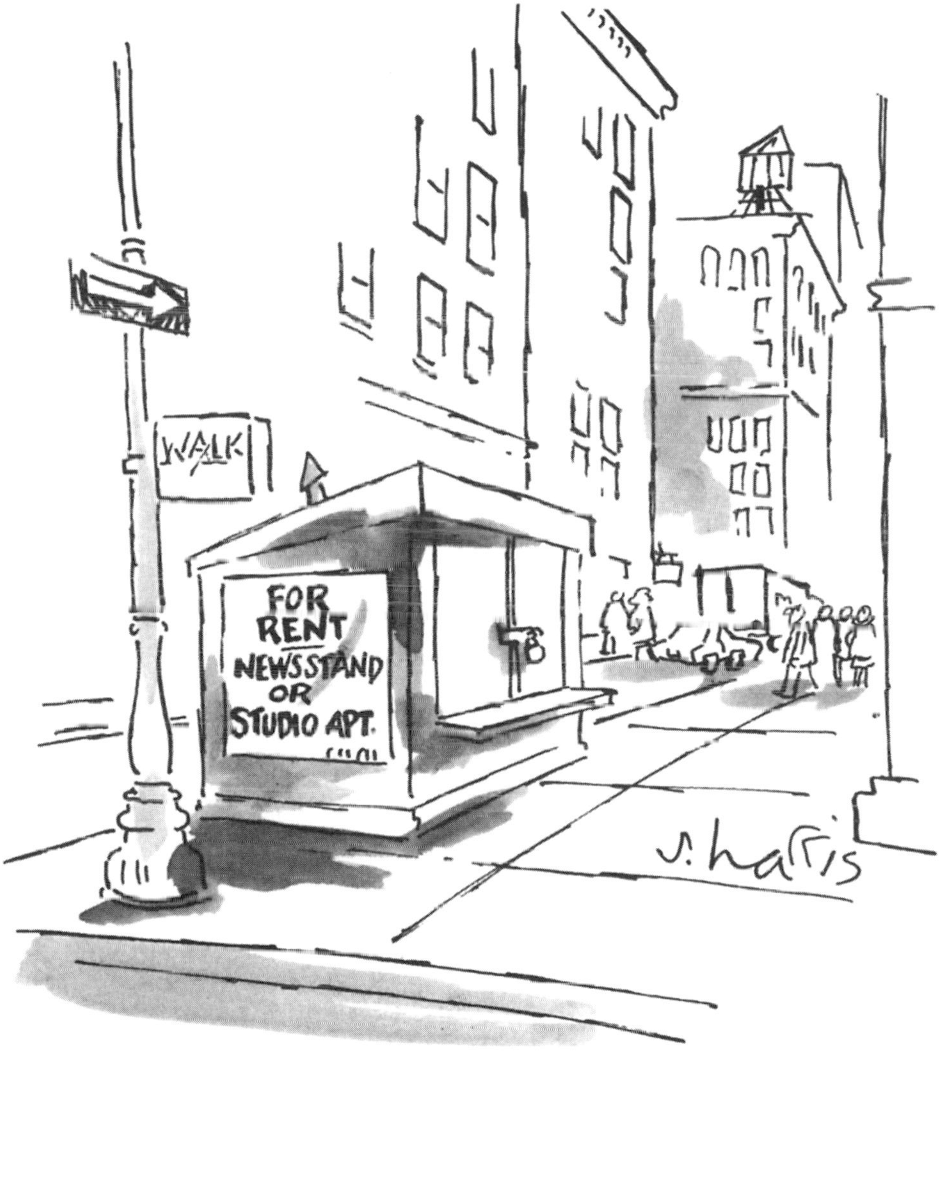
WALK
FOR RENT
NEWSSTAND
OR
STUDIO APT.
J. harris

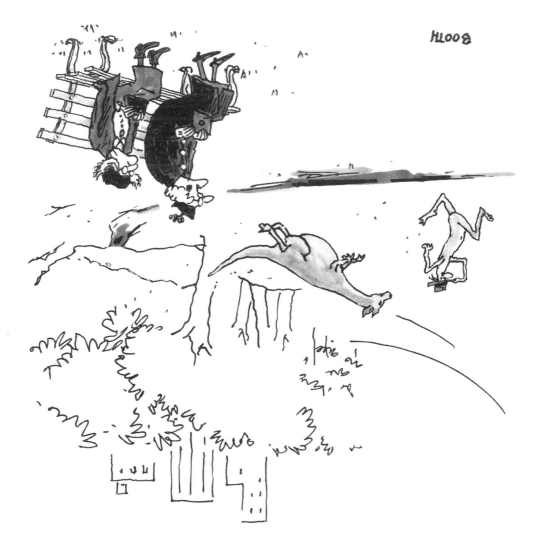

"*I love this town!*"

BOOTH

HEY! THANKS!
MStevens

OUT-OF-TOWNER

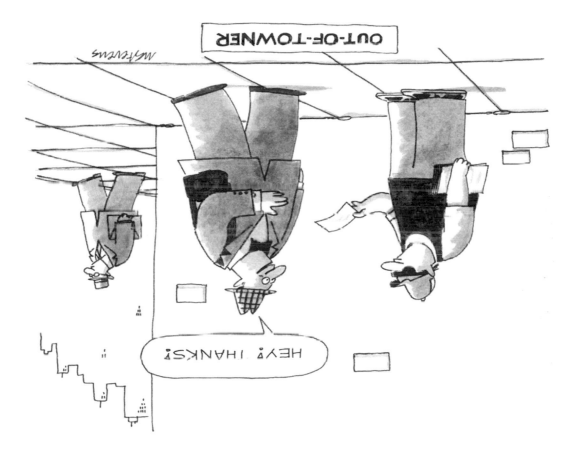

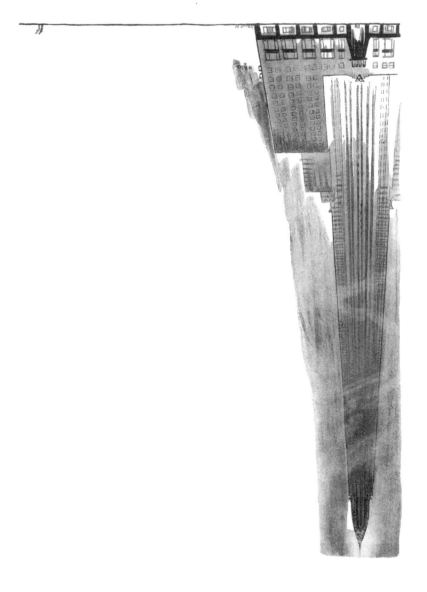

"Gives the impression of height, doesn't it?"

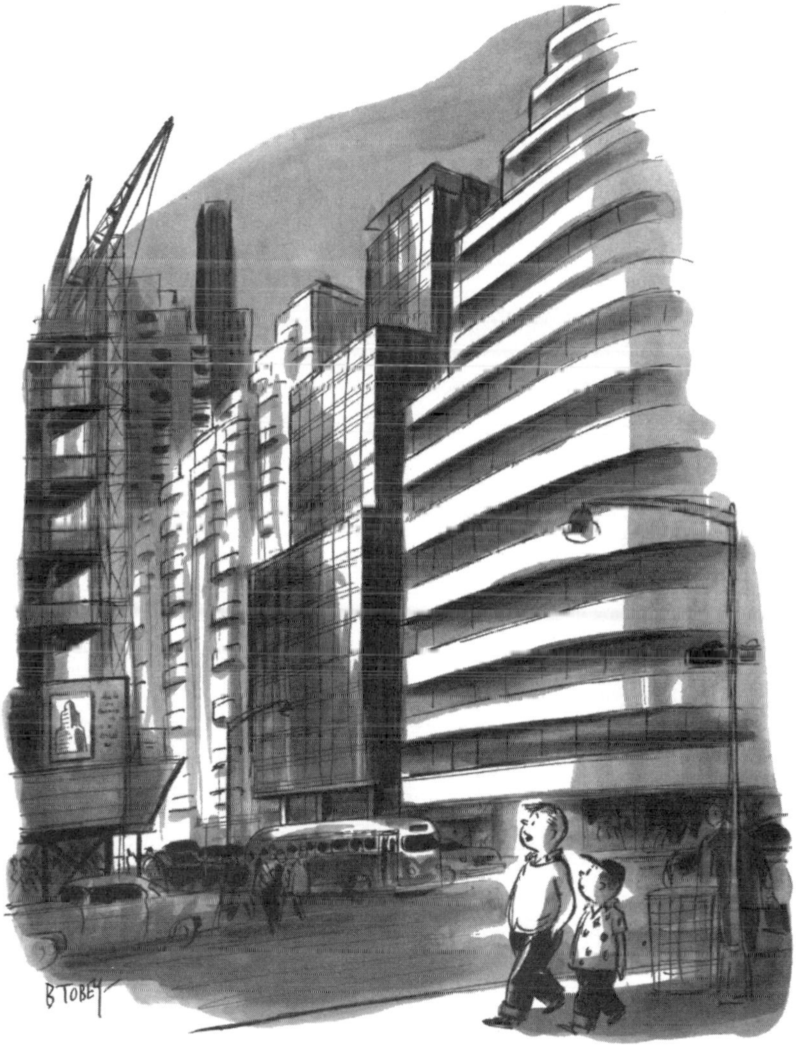
B TOBEY

"This neighborhood sure has changed since I was a kid."

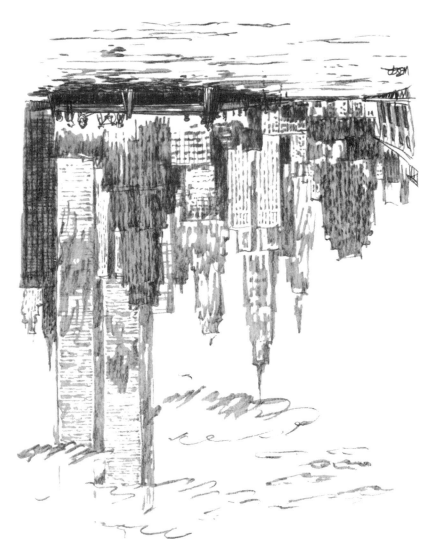

"The thing I like about New York, Claudia, is you."

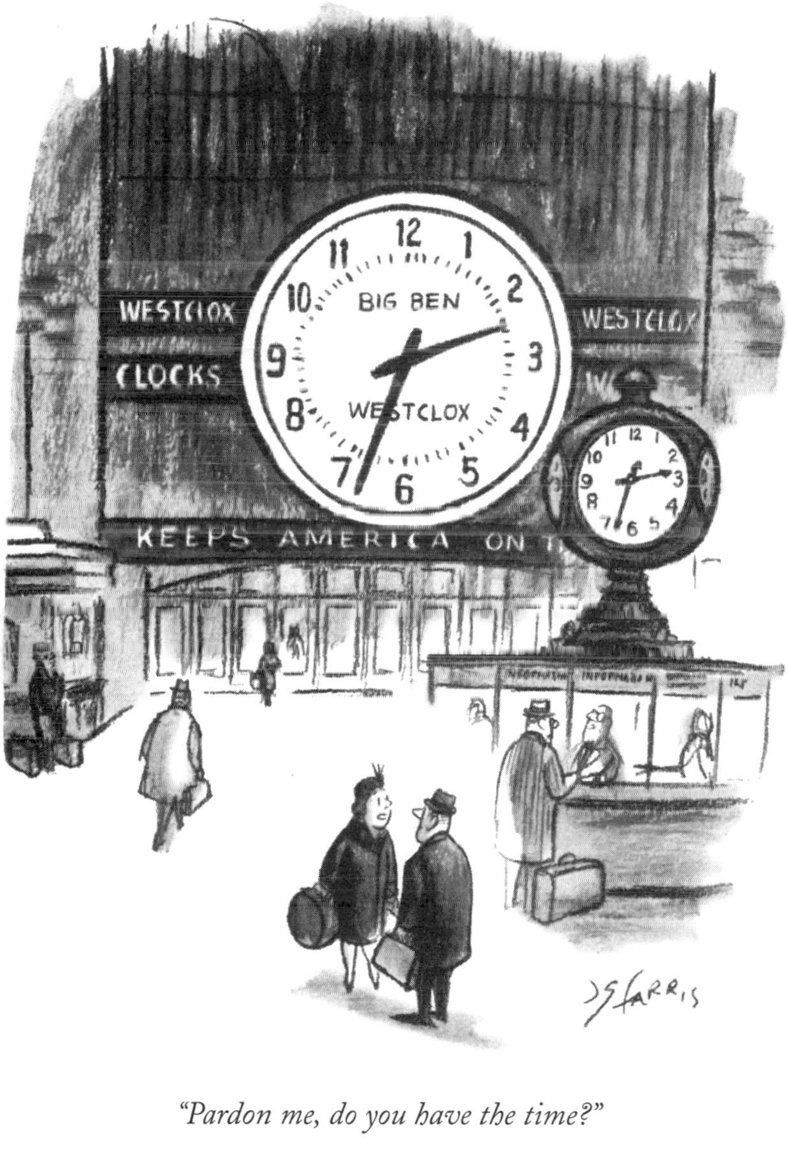
WESTCLOX
CLOCKS
BIG BEN
WESTCLOX
WESTCLOX
KEEPS AMERICA ON T

"Pardon me, do you have the time?"

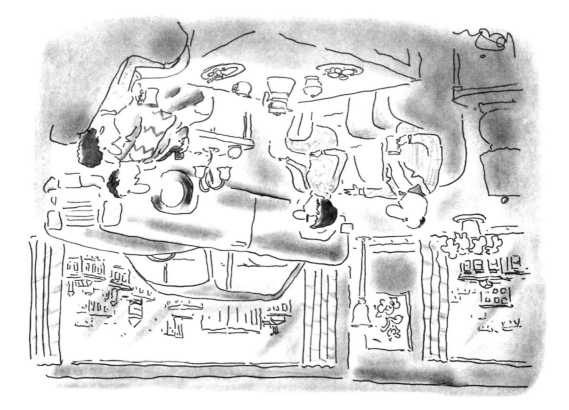

"When we moved back into the city, we decided to keep the car."

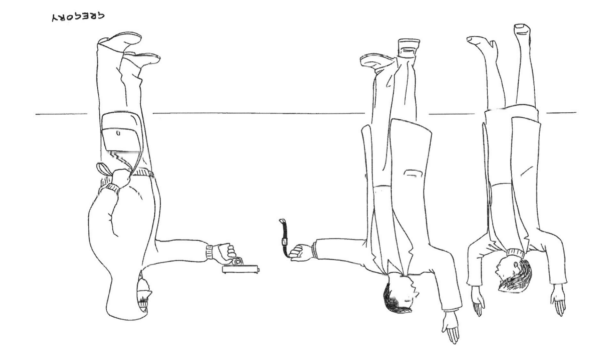

"God, I feel like such a tourist."

GREGORY

"What a day! A brilliant sun, an azure sky, the air like vintage wine!
By George, I've half a mind to do a bit of profit taking!"

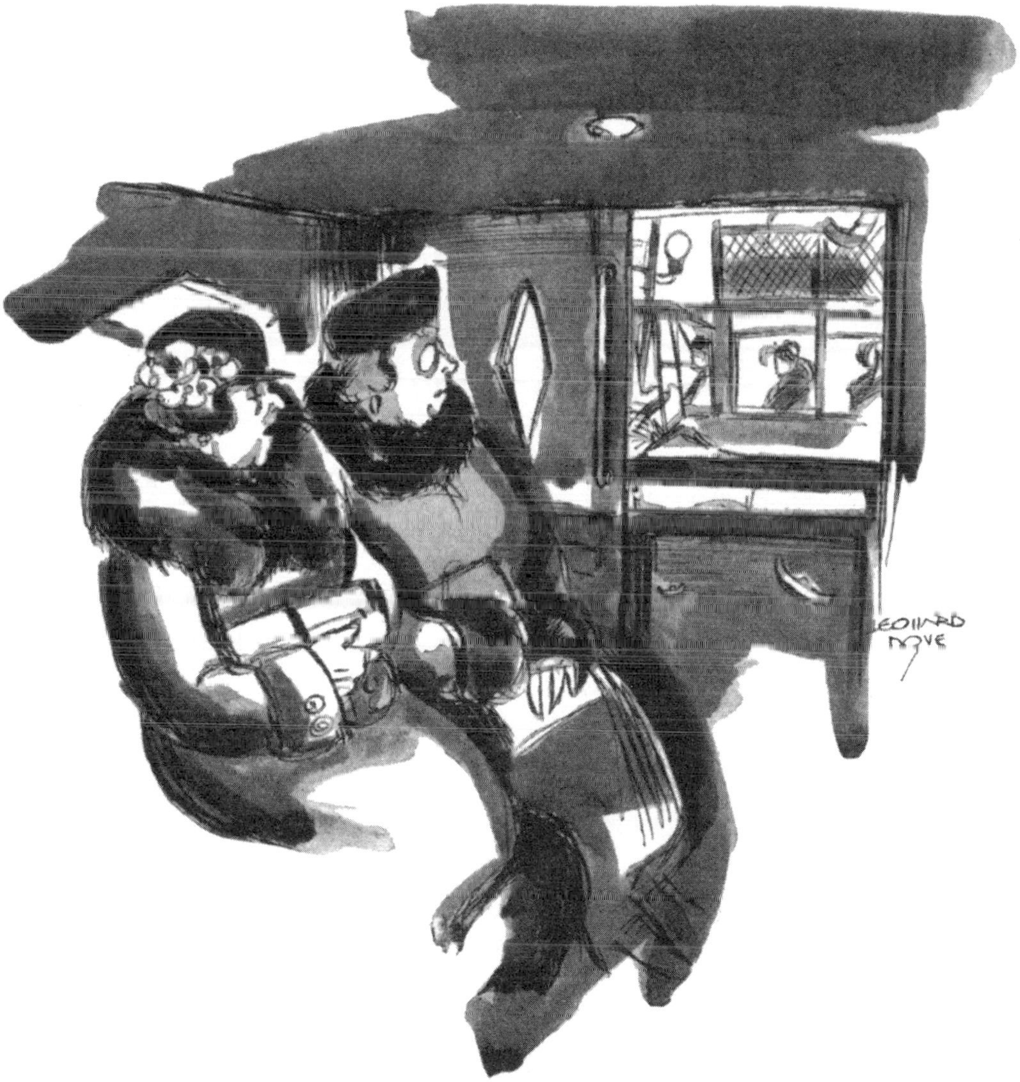
LEONARD DOVE

"I think this New York traffic is terrible. If this had been in any other city we would have been at Times Square long before now."

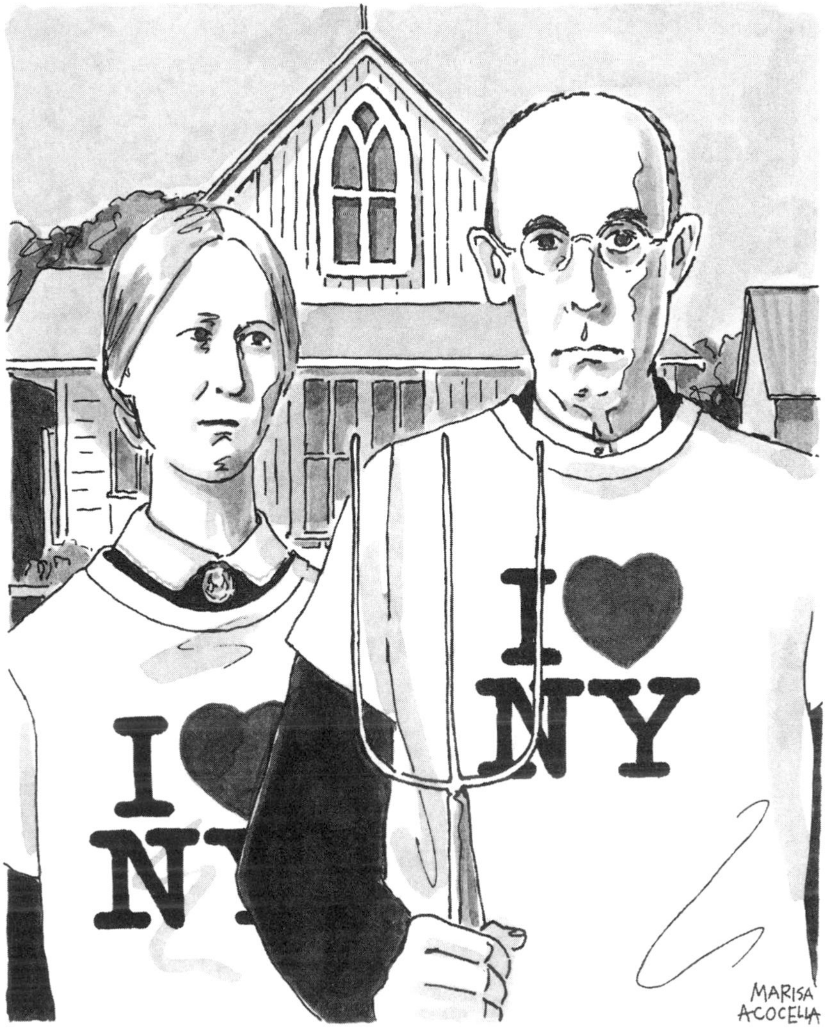
I ♥ NY
I ♥ NY
MARISA ACOCELLA

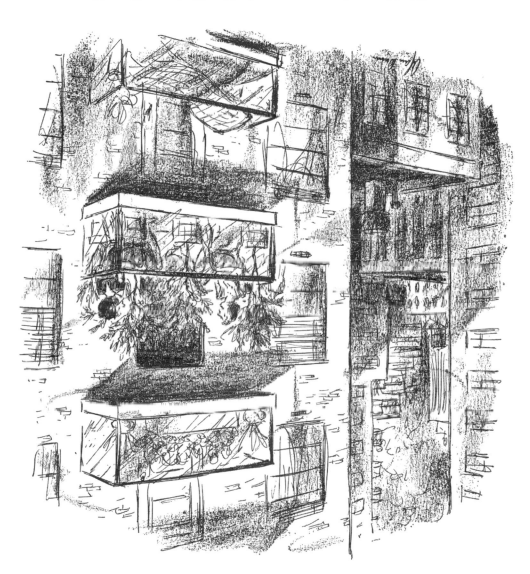

"You'd never know you were in New York, would you?"

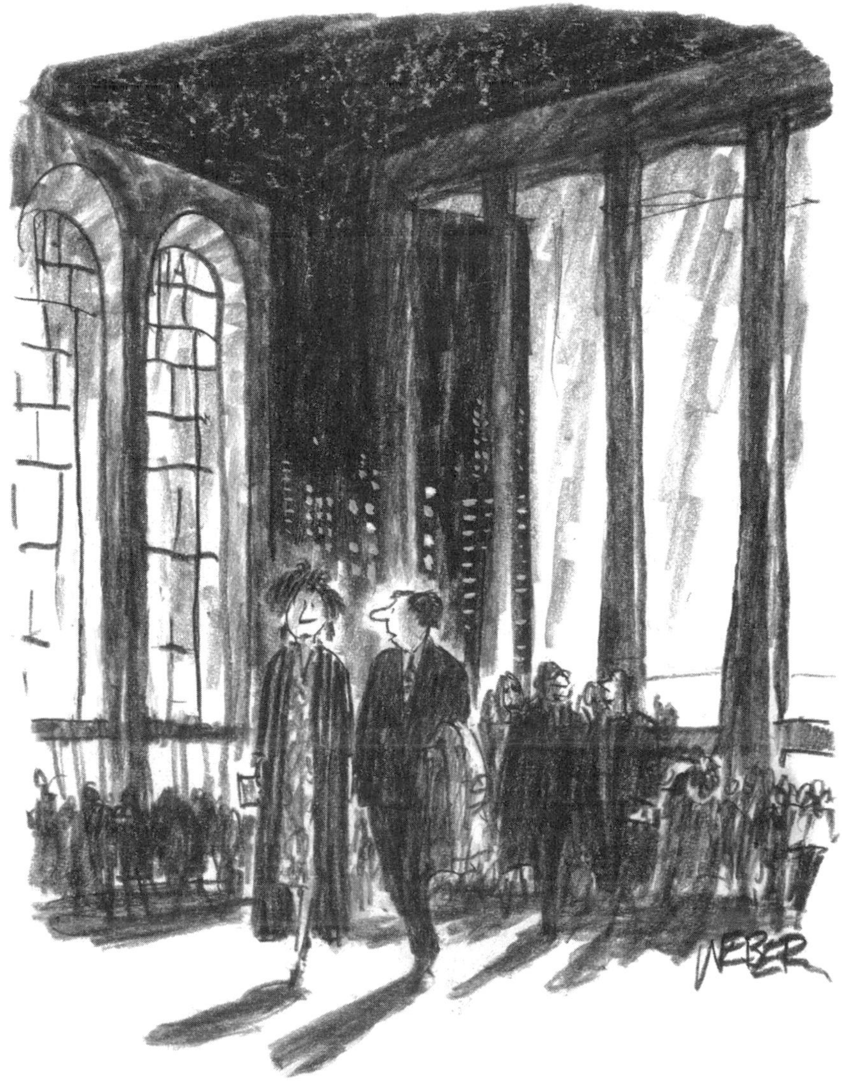
WEBER

"The music was so loud I couldn't hear myself talk."

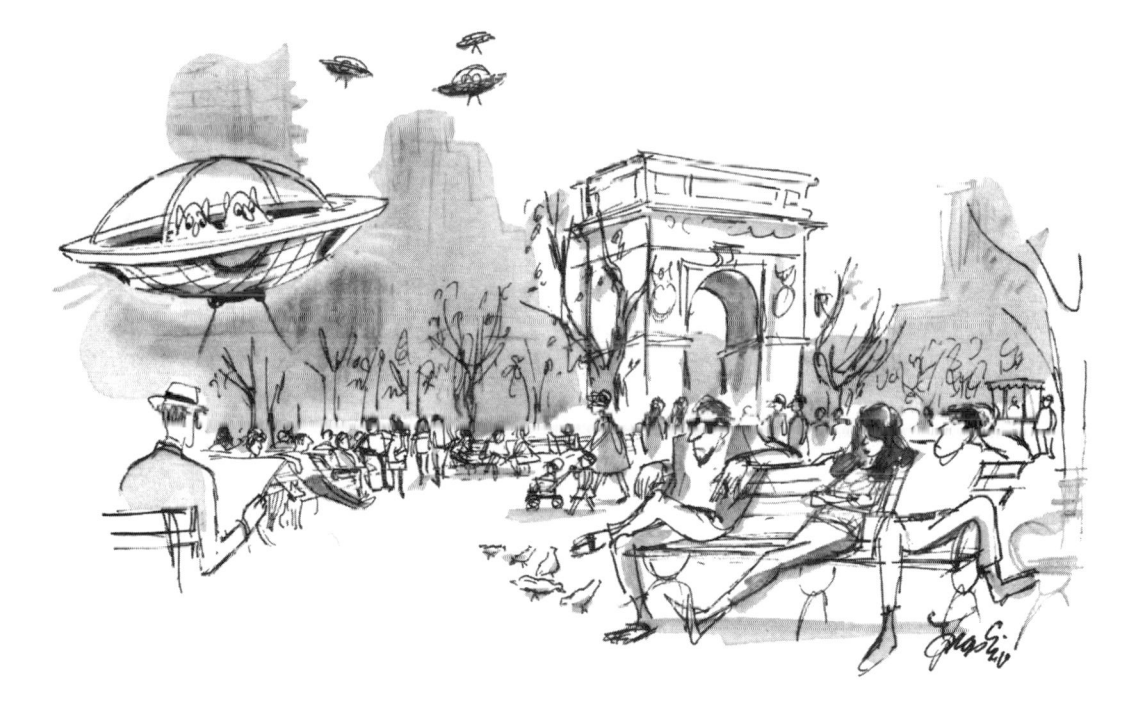

"I don't understand it. They loved us in Michigan."

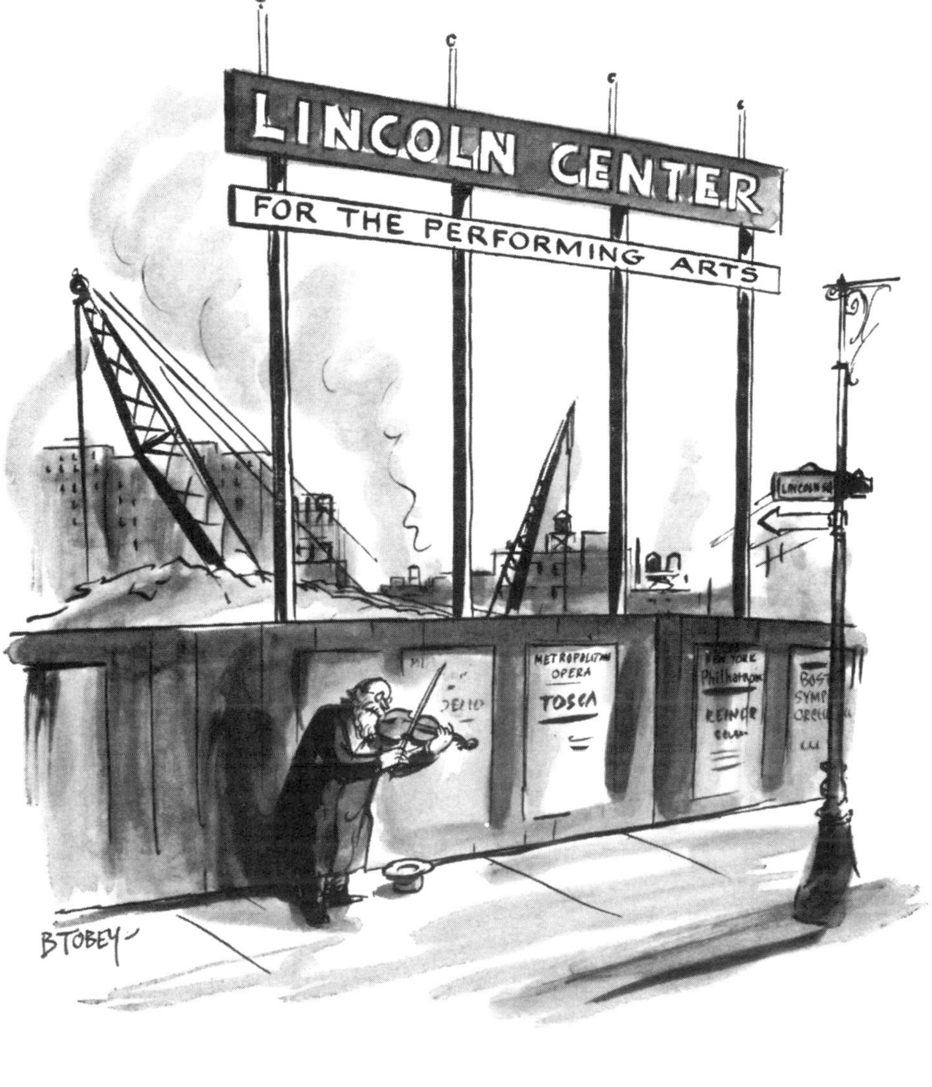
LINCOLN CENTER
FOR THE PERFORMING ARTS
METROPOLITAN
OPERA
TOSCA
NEW YORK
Philharmonic
REINER
BTOBEY

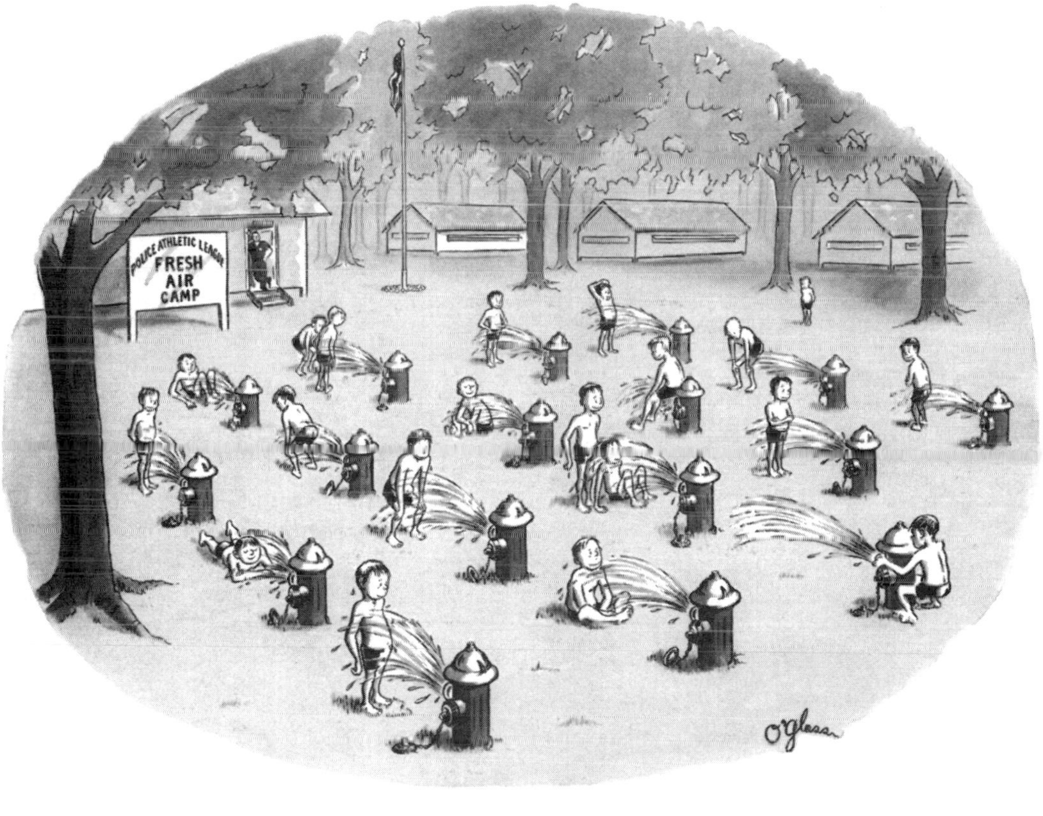
POLICE ATHLETIC LEAGUE
FRESH
AIR
CAMP
O'Glass

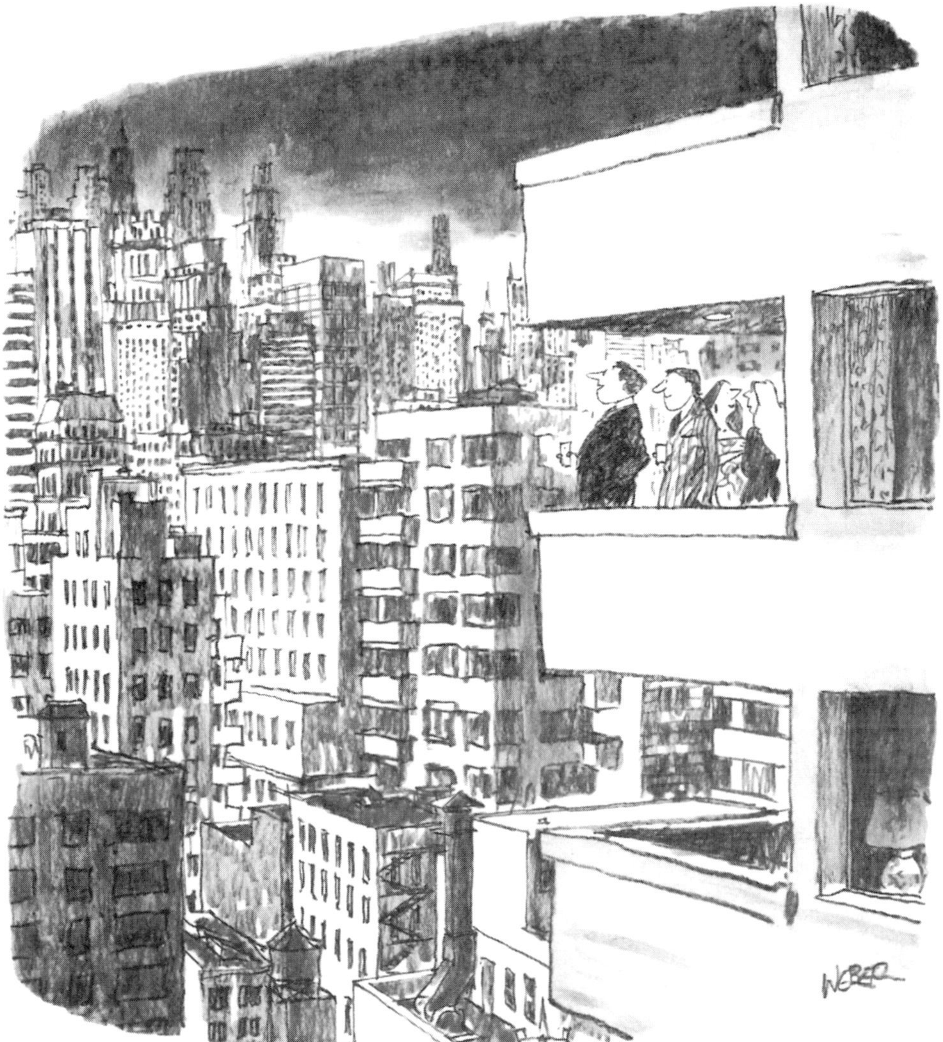
WEBER

"We love the view. It helps to remind us that we're part of a larger community."

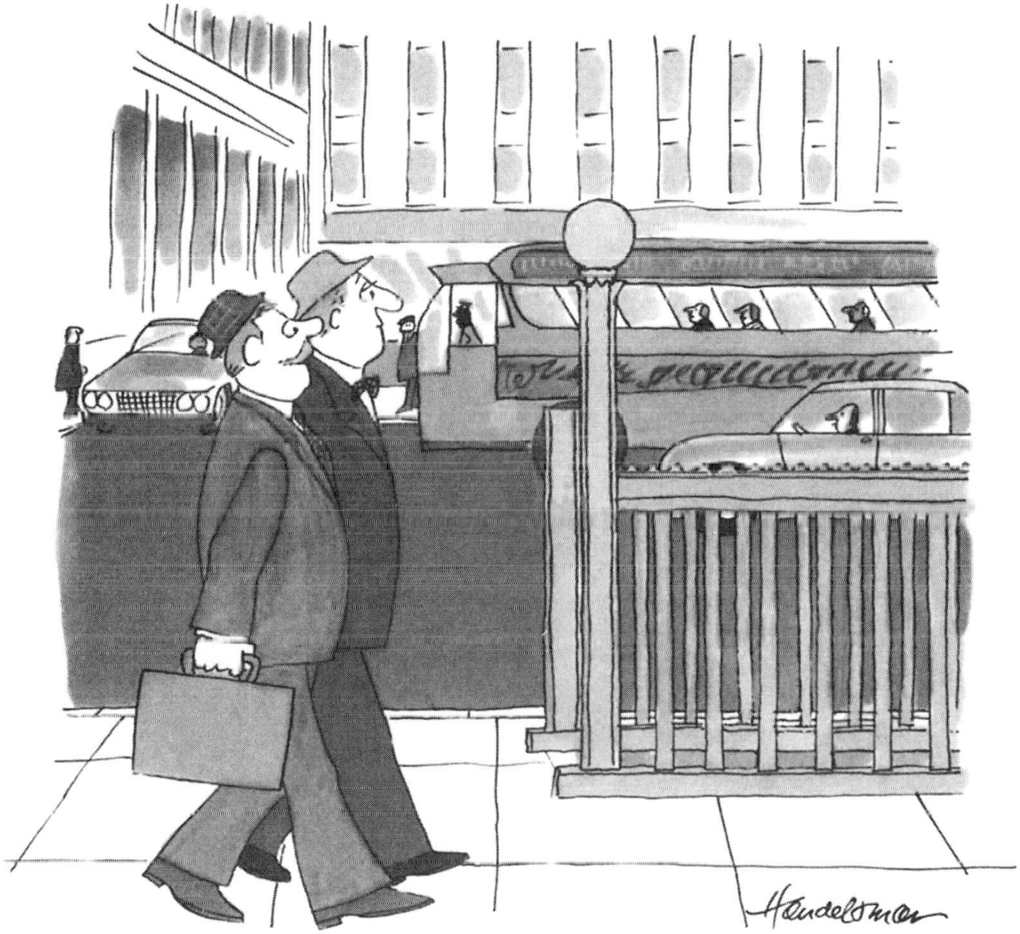
Handelsman

"It's a hell of a town, though, Bill. I never cease to marvel at the fact that the Bronx is up and the Battery's down."

"I used to think it was cruel to keep a dog in the city, but Homer's made a remarkable adjustment."

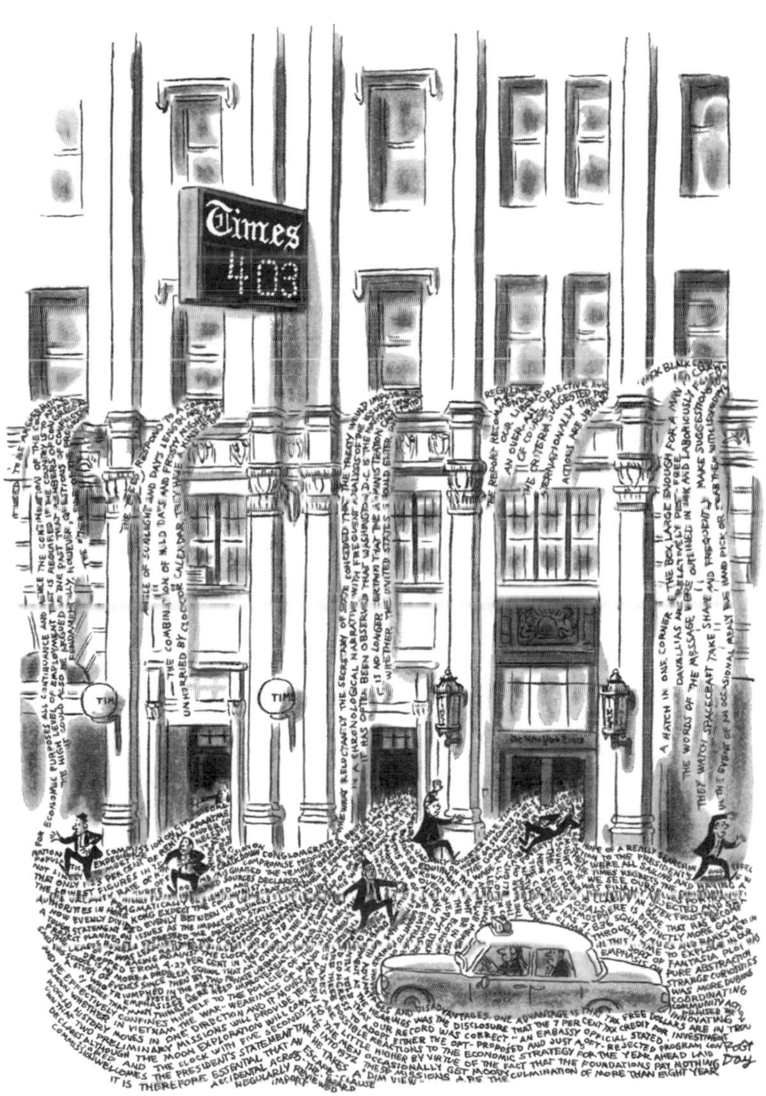
Times
403

CROSS CITY
EXPRESSWAY
VIABLE
ALTERNATIVE
Koren

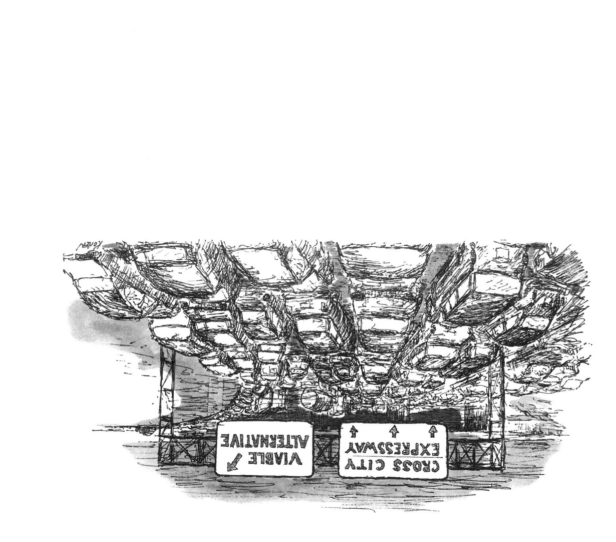

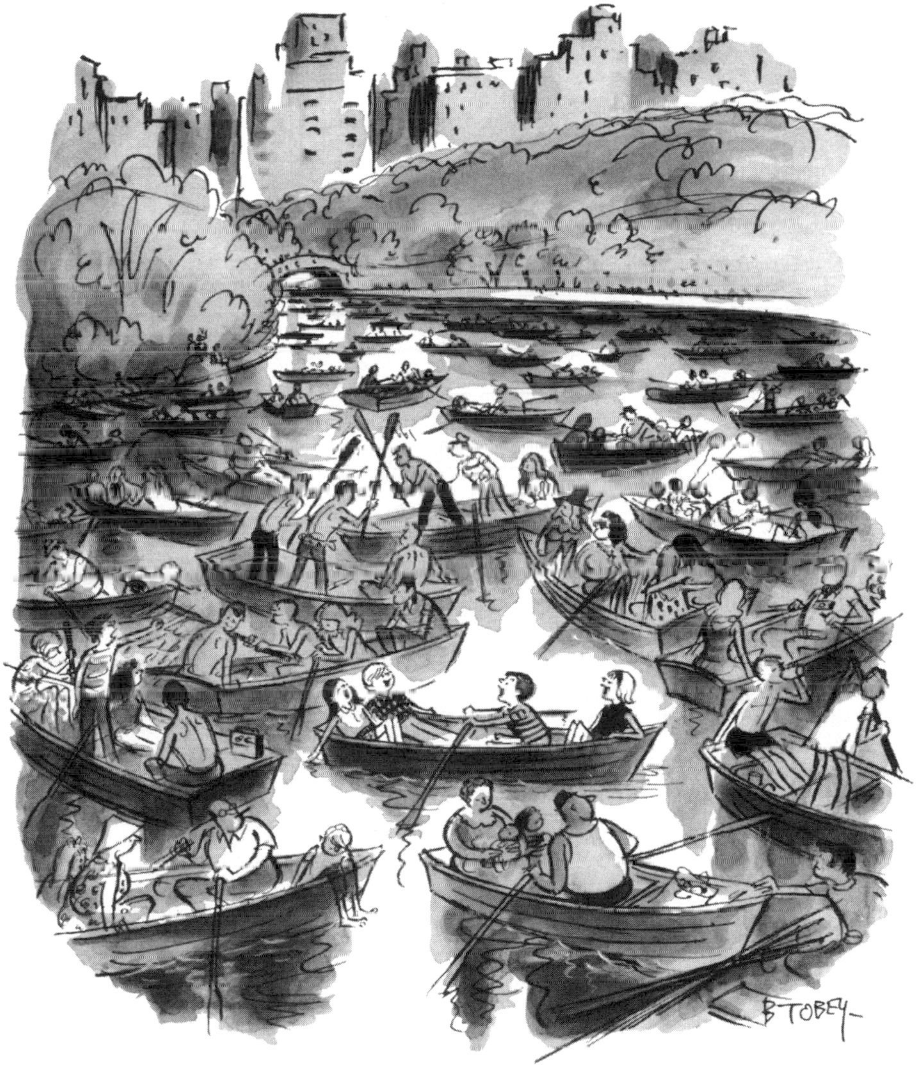
B TOBEY

"Row, row, row your boat, gently down the stream. Merrily, merrily, merrily, merrily…"

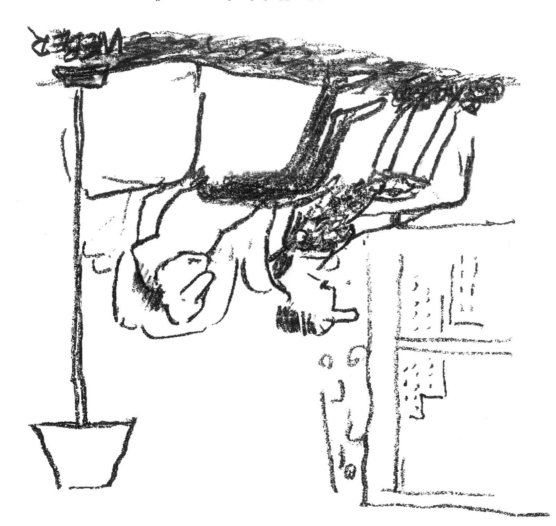

"Nothing beats New York for sheer energy."

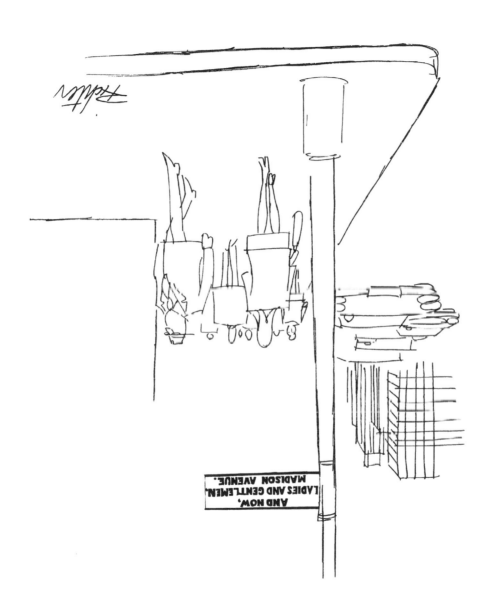

AND NOW,
LADIES AND GENTLEMEN,
MADISON AVENUE.

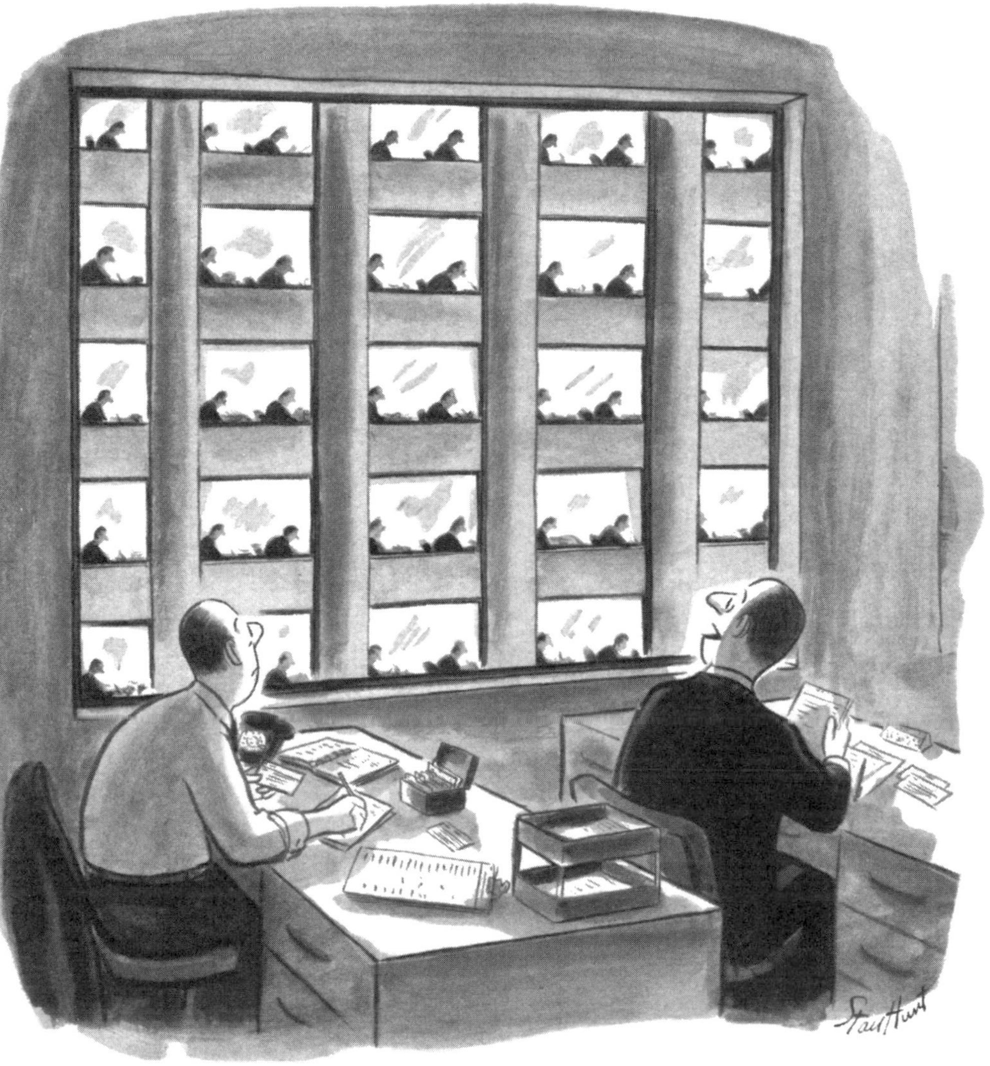
Stan Hunt

"Poor things!"

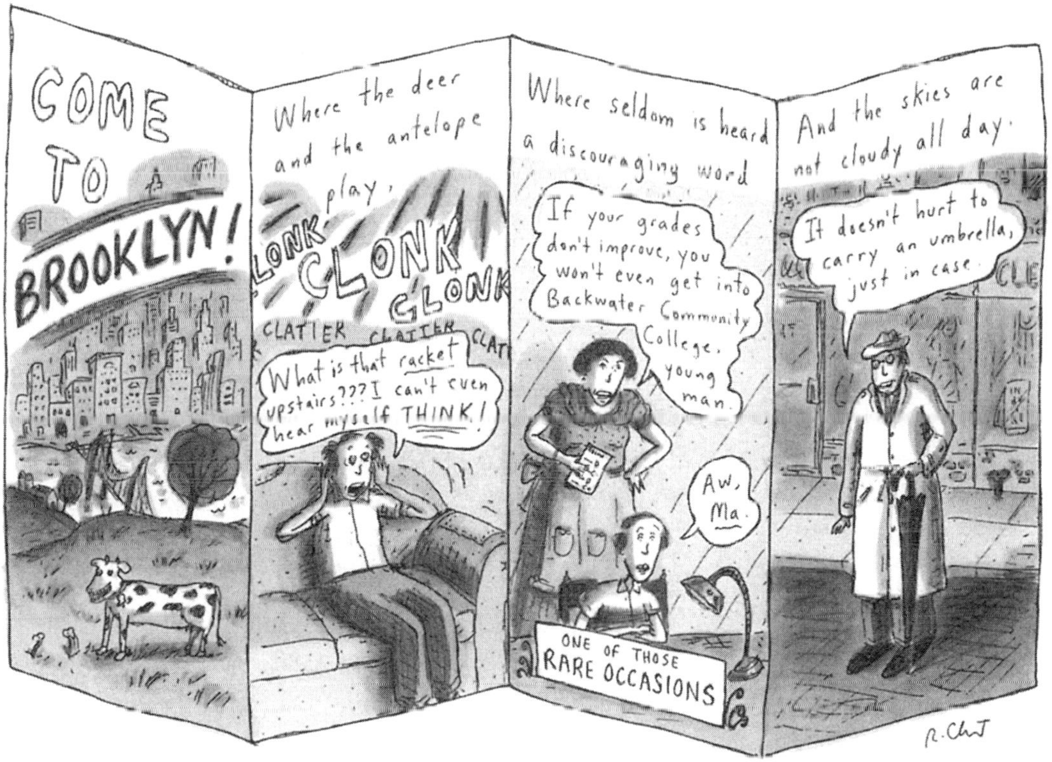
COME TO BROOKLYN!
Where the deer and the antelope play,
LONK CLONK CLONK
CLATTER CLATTER CLATT
What is that racket upstairs??? I can't even hear myself THINK!
Where seldom is heard a discouraging word
If your grades don't improve, you won't even get into Backwater Community College, young man.
Aw, Ma.
ONE OF THOSE RARE OCCASIONS
And the skies are not cloudy all day.
It doesn't hurt to carry an umbrella, just in case.
R. Chast

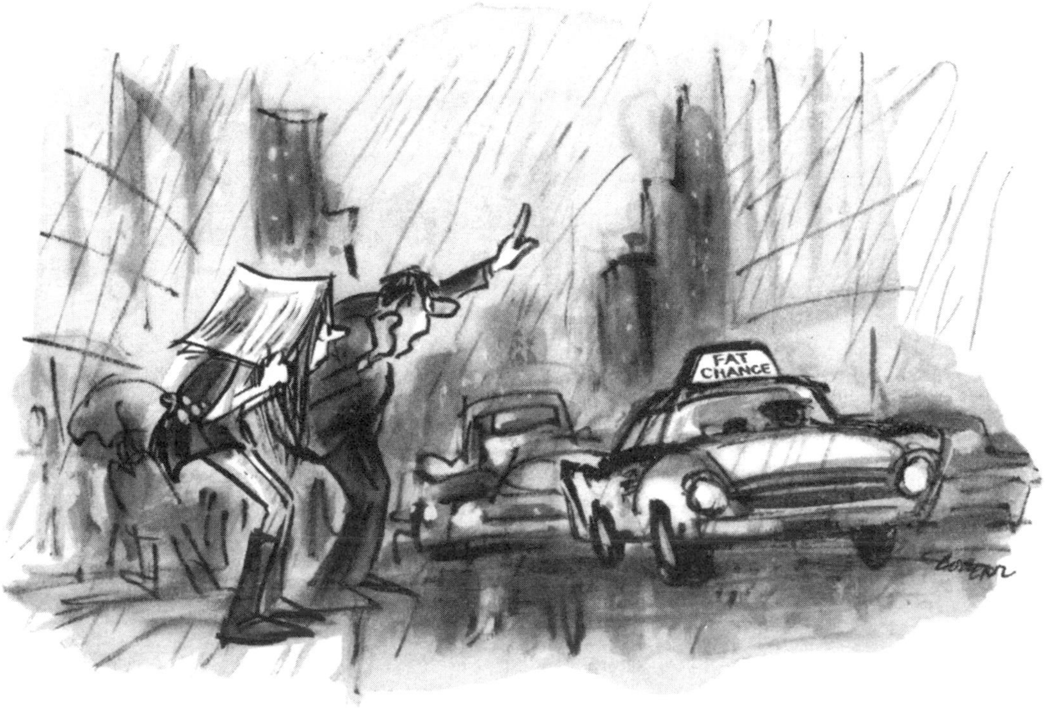
FAT CHANCE

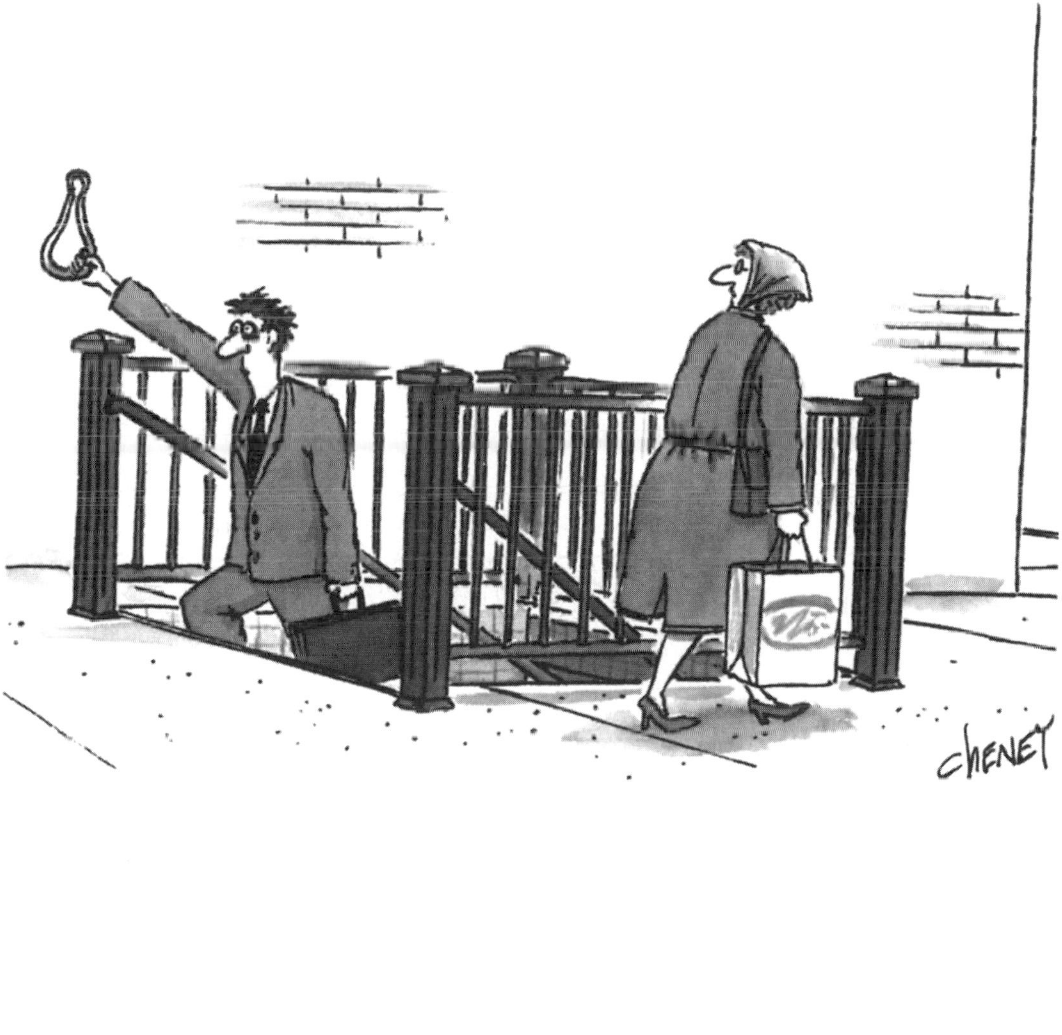
CHENEY

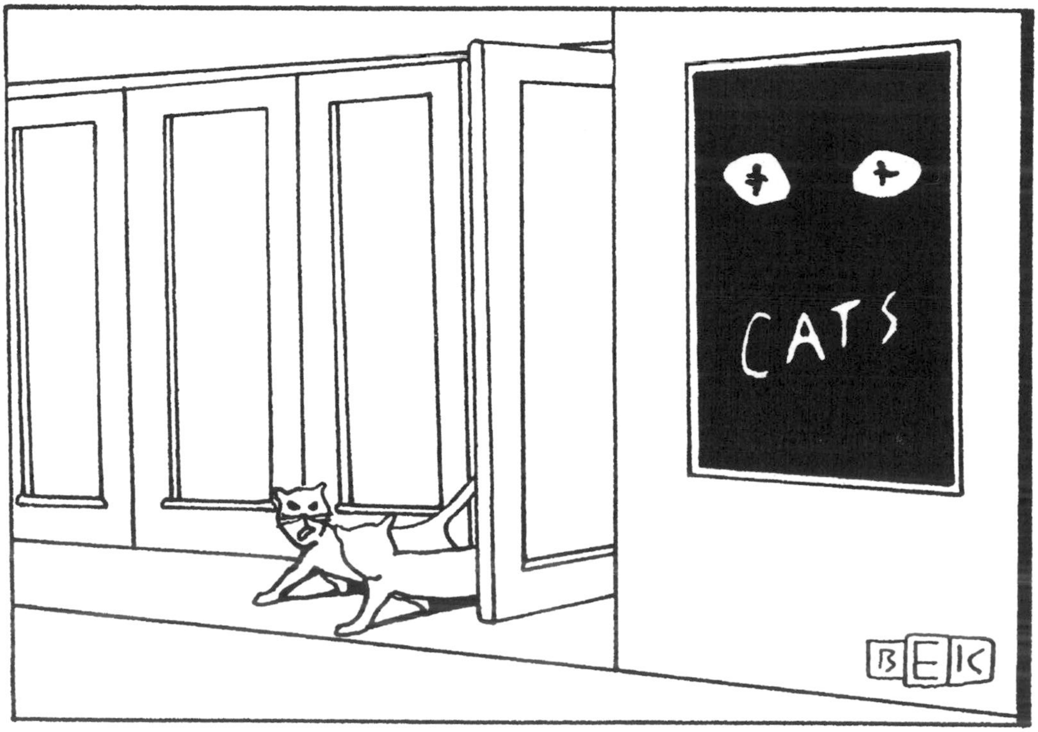
CATS
BEK

"It was so depressing. When I go to the theatre, I want to be entertained."

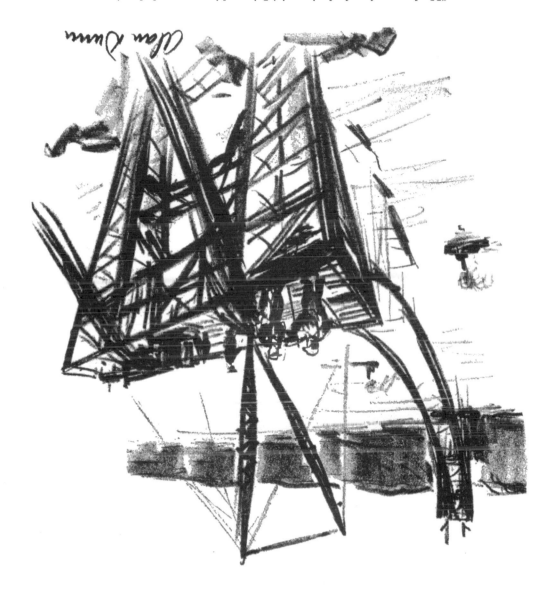

"Yeah, once break the ice wit' Joisey this way and there's no tellin' what'll happen."

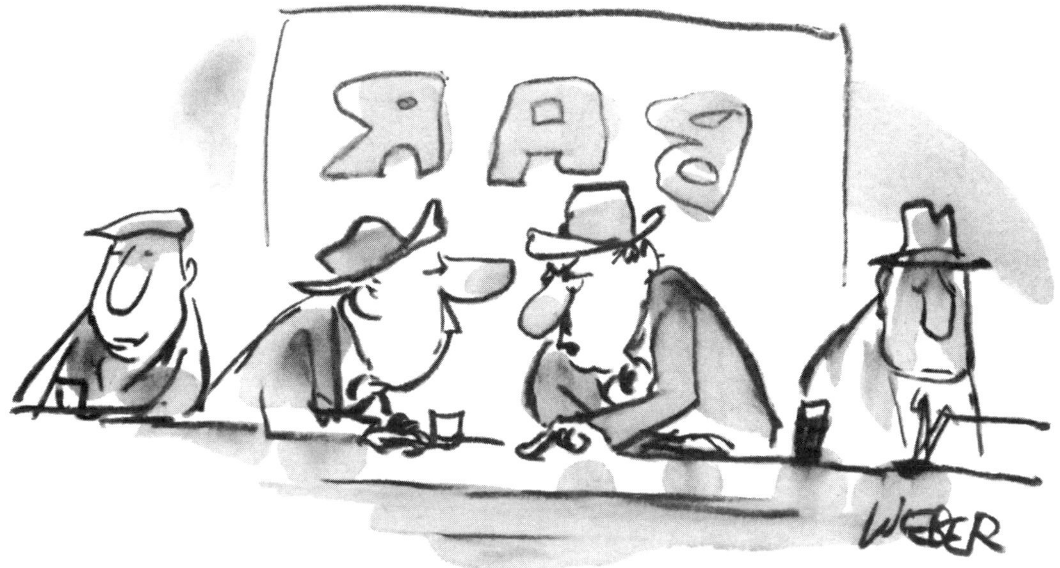
WEBER

"The first step toward solving New York City's problems is to <u>state</u> them, which I will now proceed to do."

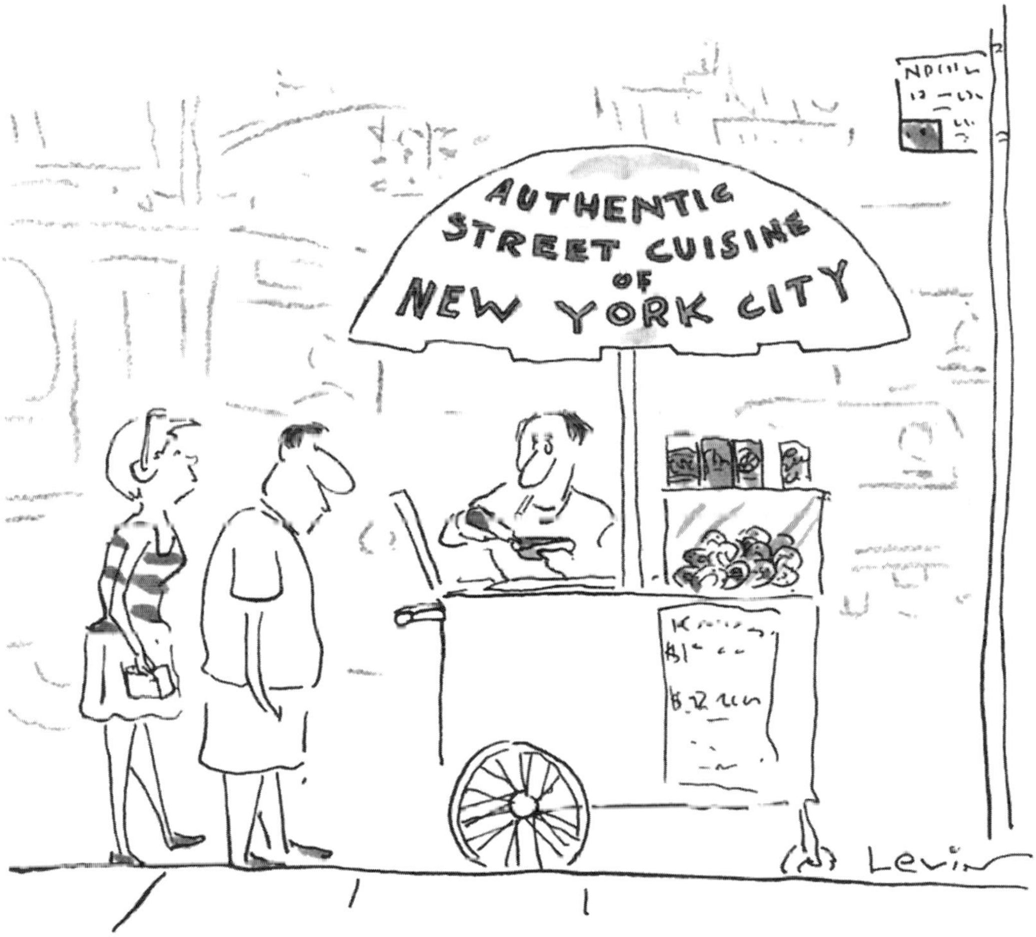
AUTHENTIC
STREET CUISINE
OF
NEW YORK CITY
Levin

"It's Brooklyn clam chowder—you got a problem with that?"

Shanahan

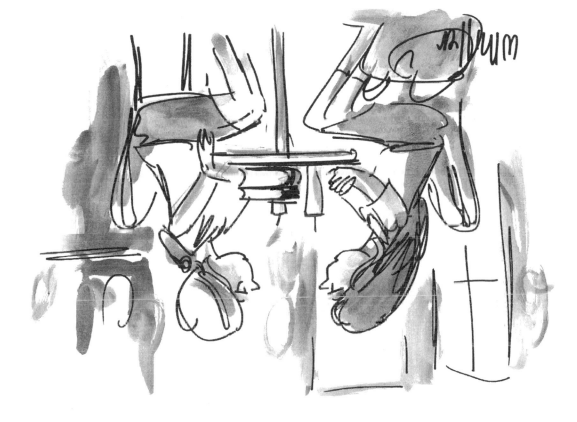

"A village did raise him. But, of course, it was Greenwich Village."

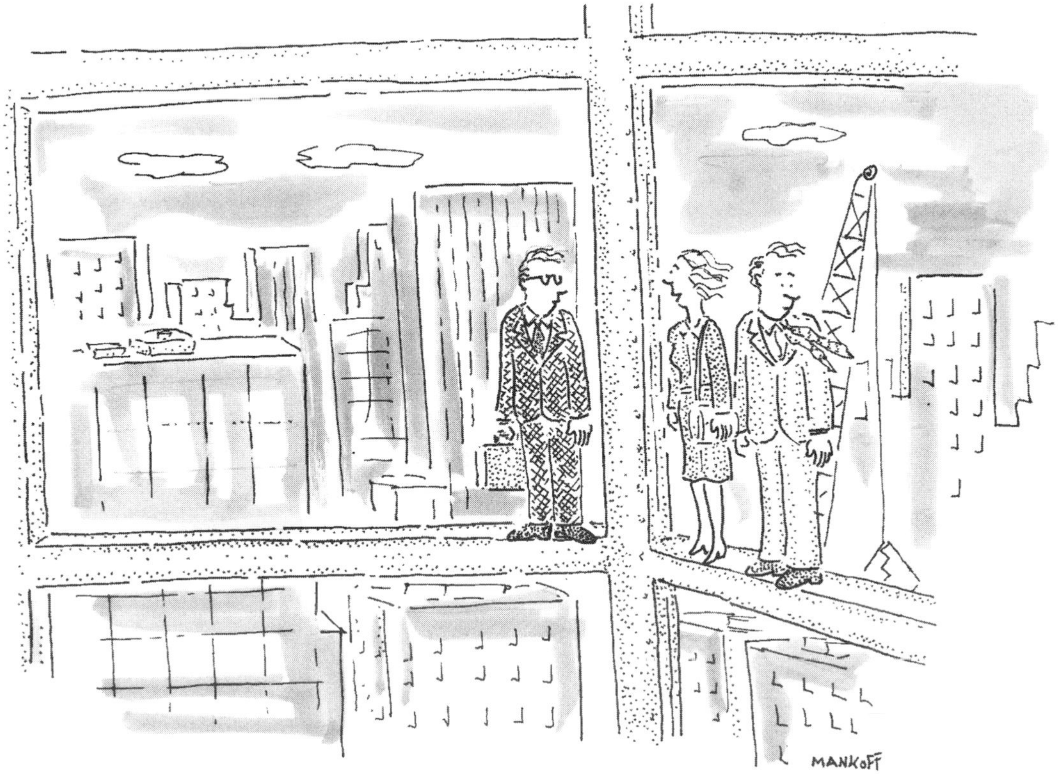
MANKOFF

"We'll take it."

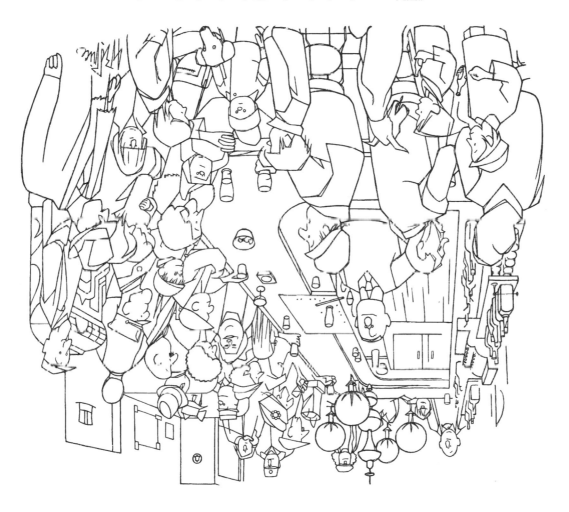

"This must be the last family bar in the Bronx."

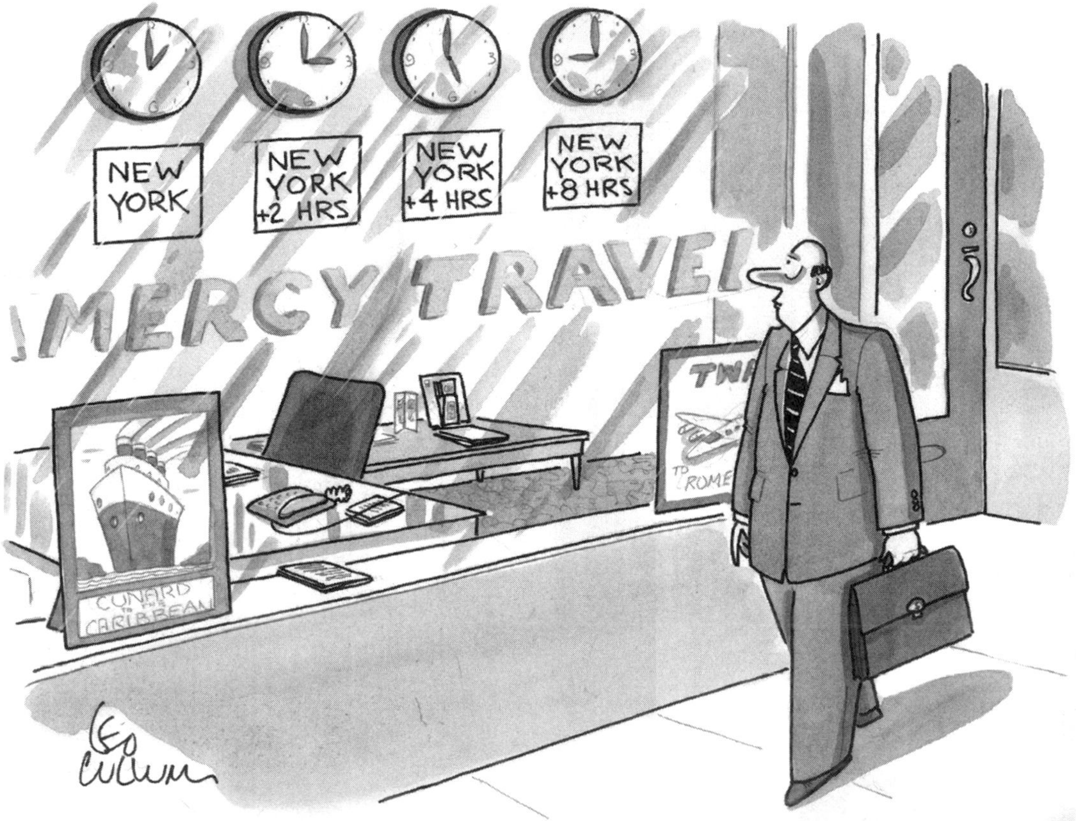
NEW YORK
NEW YORK +2 HRS
NEW YORK +4 HRS
NEW YORK +8 HRS
MERCY TRAVEL
CUNARD TO THE CARIBBEAN
TWA
TO ROME

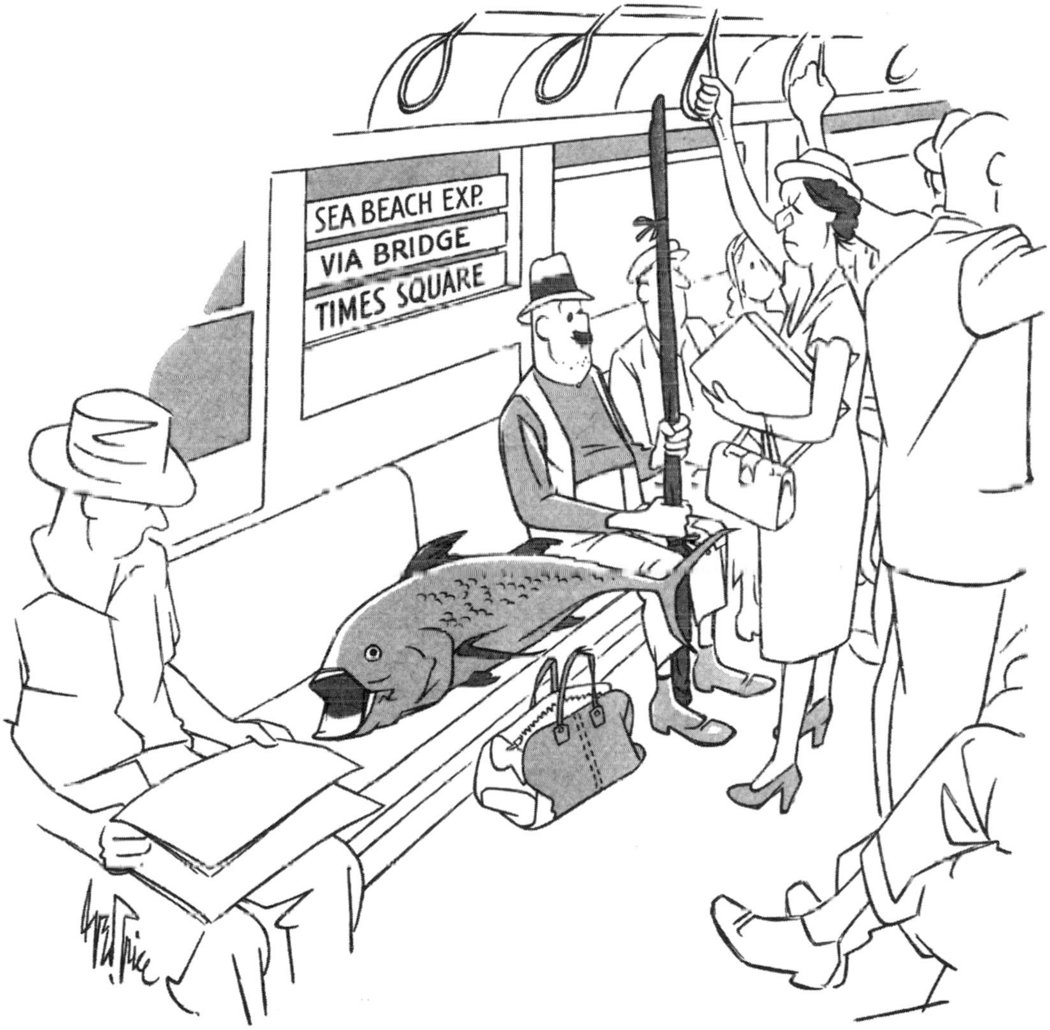
SEA BEACH EXP.
VIA BRIDGE
TIMES SQUARE

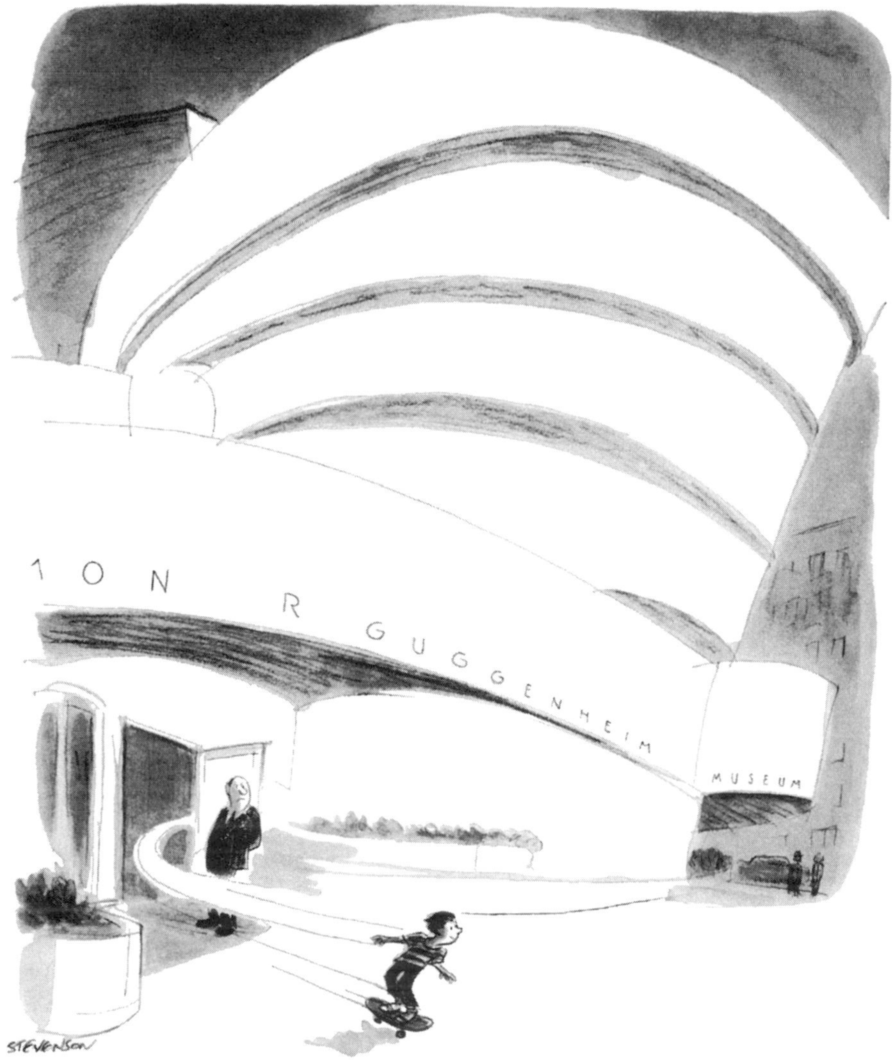
1ON R GUGGENHEIM
MUSEUM
STEVENSON

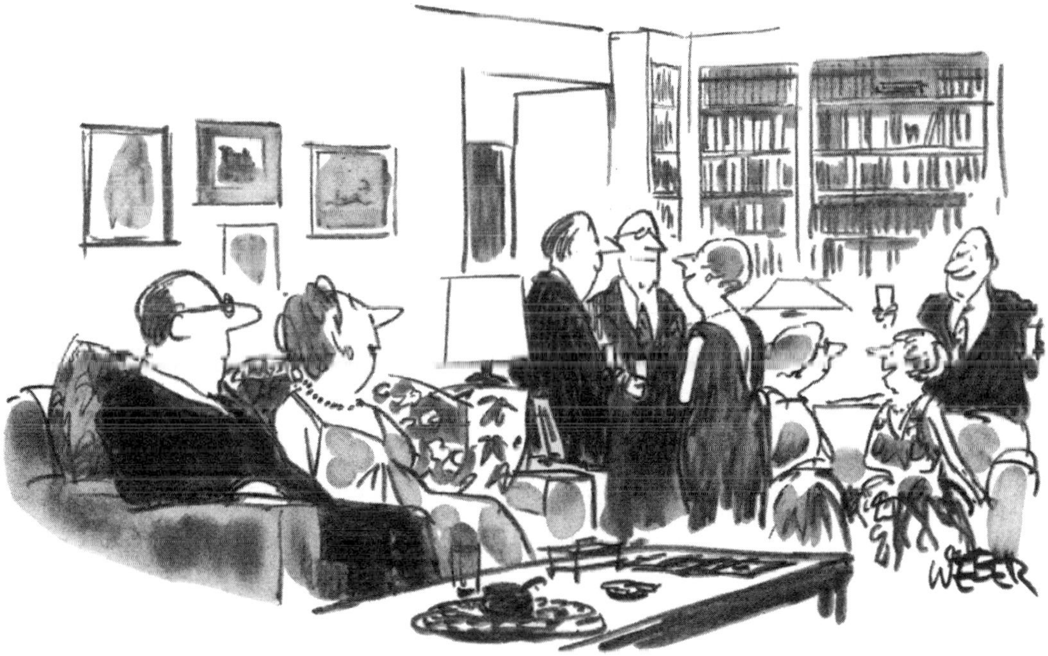
WEBER

"Louise and Greg are from Pittsburgh, Richard and Beth are from Boston, you and Ellen are from Hartford, and Glen and I are from Detroit. Goodness! New York certainly <u>*is*</u> *a melting pot!"*

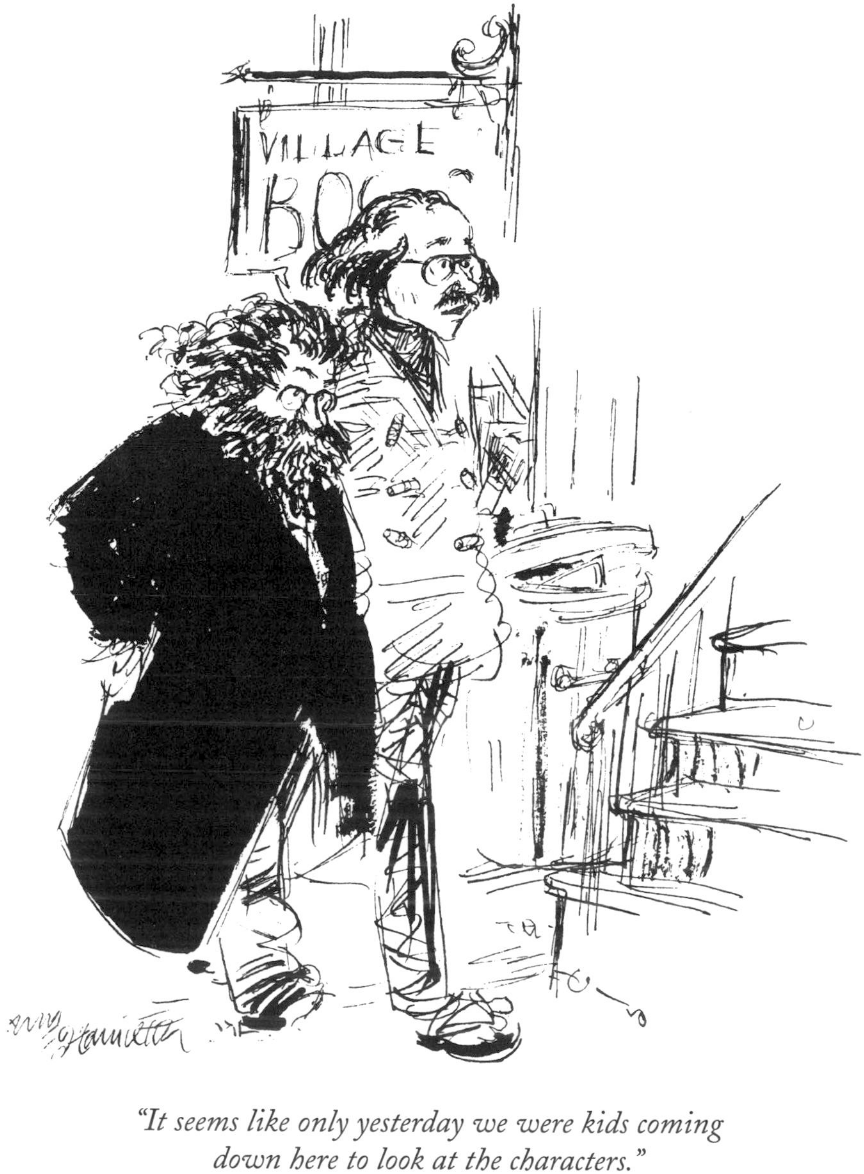
VILLAGE
BO

"It seems like only yesterday we were kids coming down here to look at the characters."

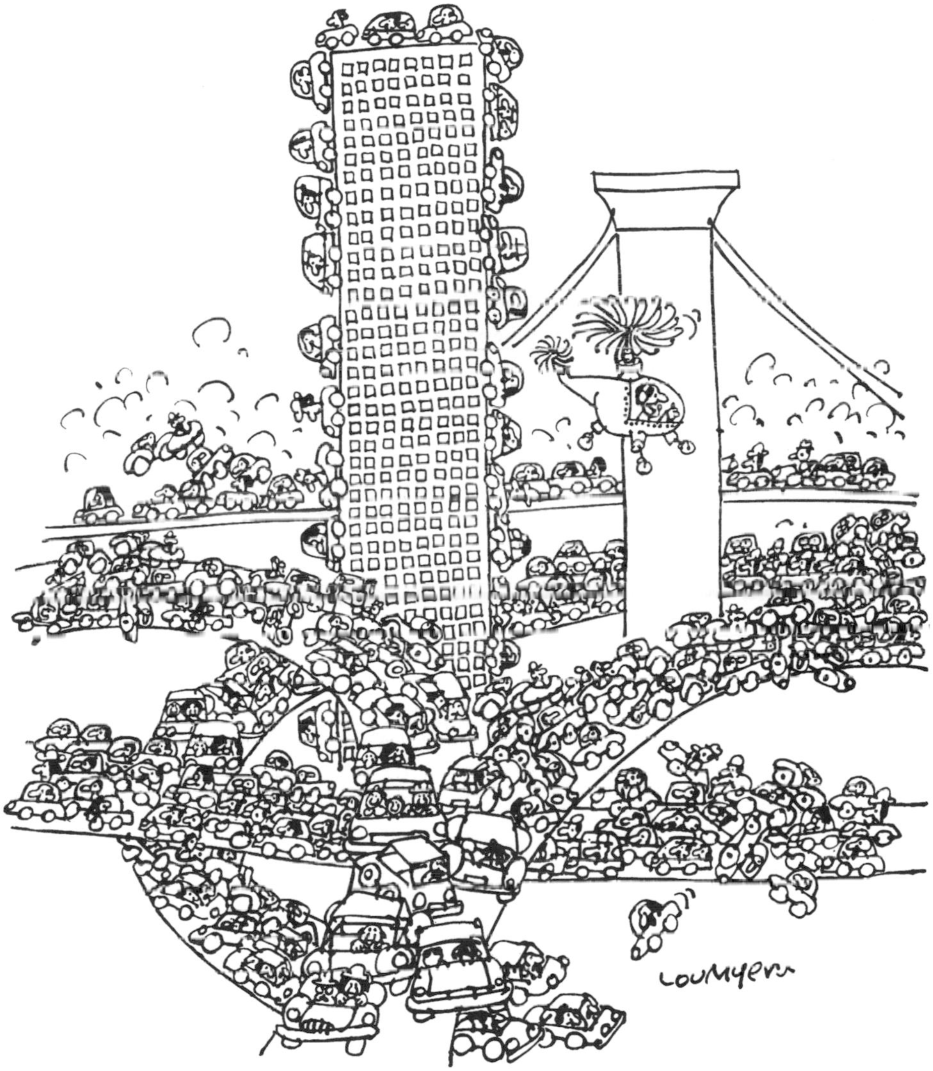
LOUMYERS

"They're bumper to bumper on the B.Q.E. The approaches to the Lincoln and Holland Tunnels are stalled, and there are rubbernecking delays on the Major Deegan."

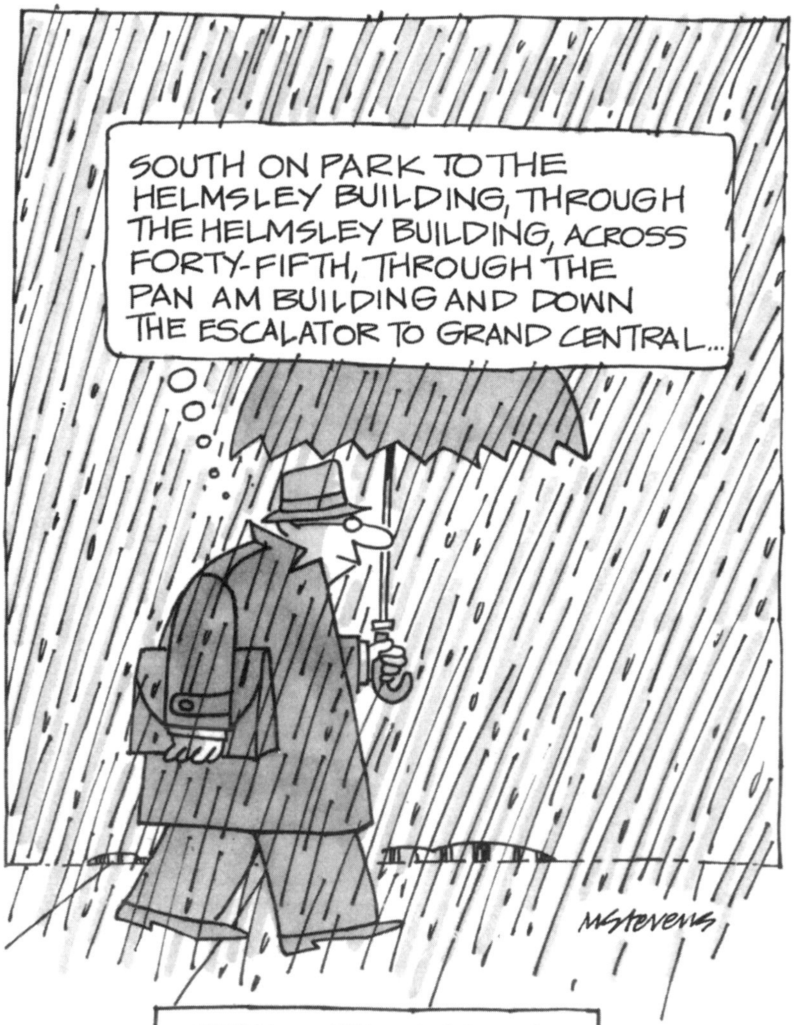
SOUTH ON PARK TO THE HELMSLEY BUILDING, THROUGH THE HELMSLEY BUILDING, ACROSS FORTY-FIFTH, THROUGH THE PAN AM BUILDING AND DOWN THE ESCALATOR TO GRAND CENTRAL...
MSTEVENS

STREET SMARTS

"You won't believe how much I was paying for an apartment this size in New York."

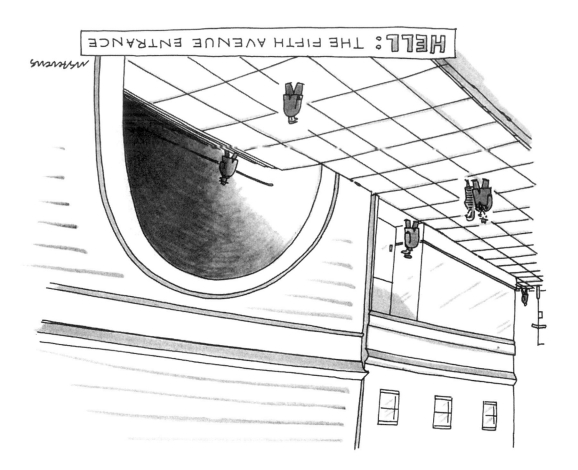

HELL: THE FIFTH AVENUE ENTRANCE

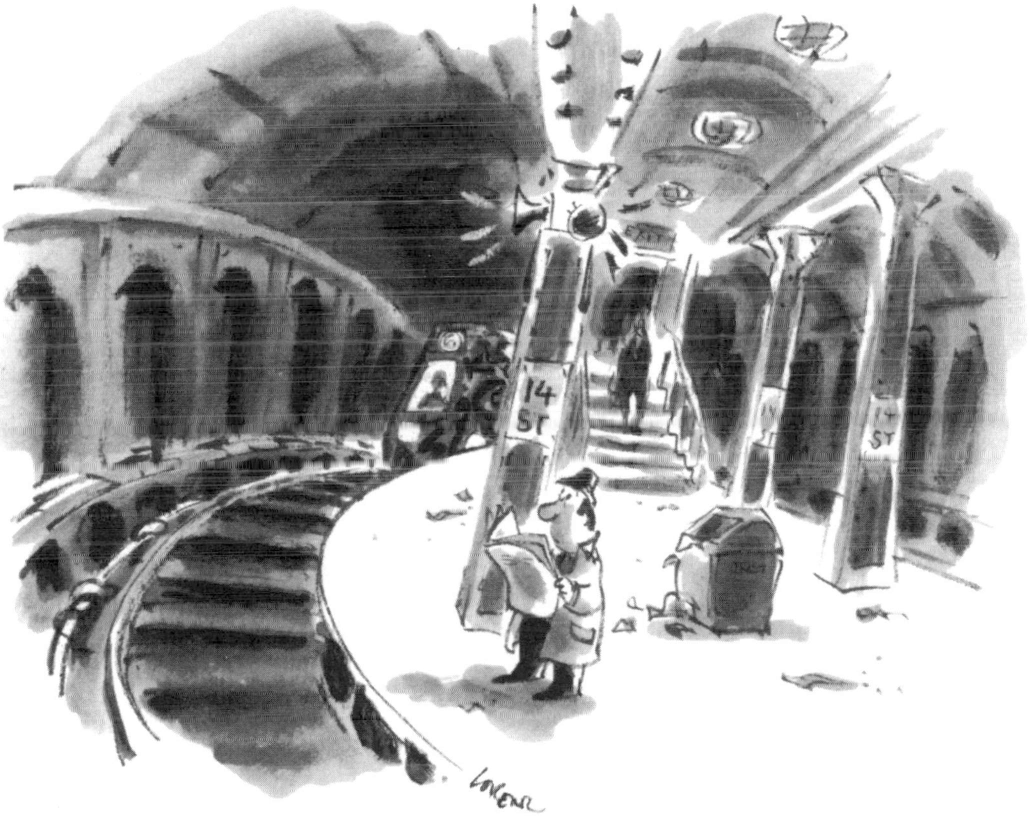
14
ST
14
ST

"Uptown local now arriving, featuring early work by Tico '88, Baco-Loco, and Zazoo 101."

"*Is everything satisfactory here—I mean as befits our one little star in the New York 'Times'?*"

GARAGE

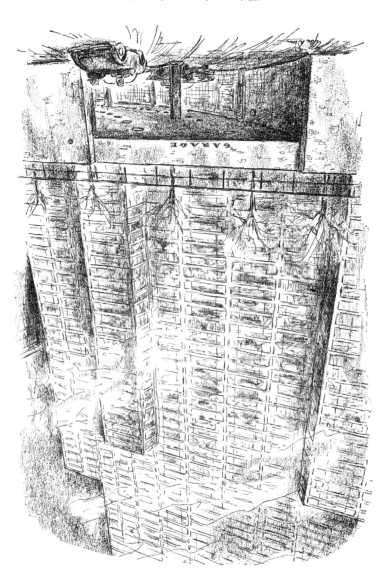

"It's good to get home!"

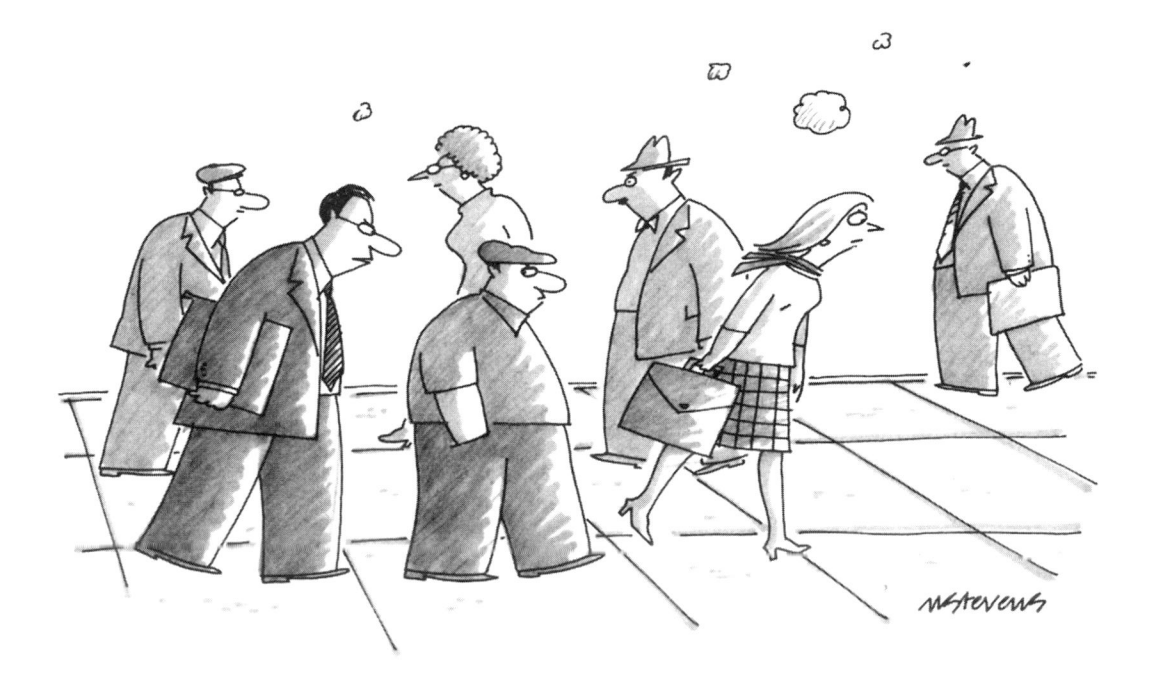

"Could you walk a little faster, buddy? This is New York."

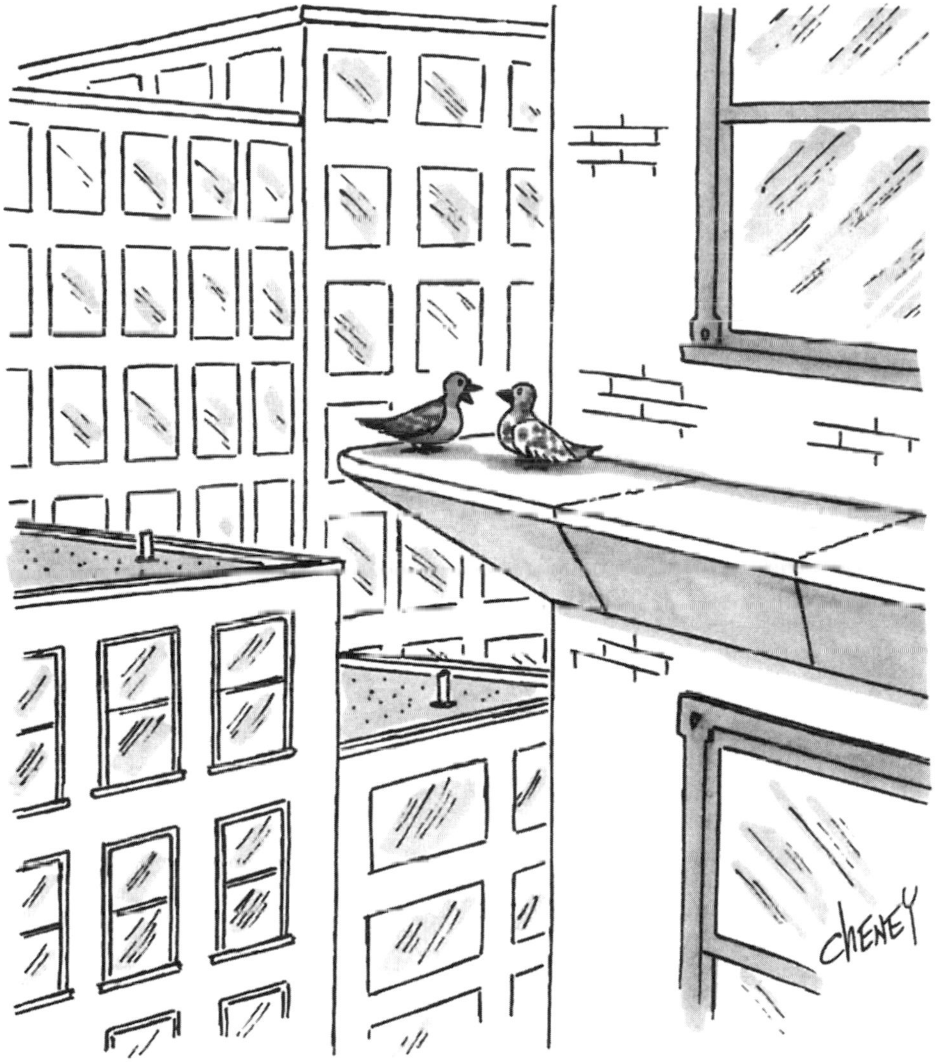
CHENEY

"Hey, this is New York, and you're a pigeon. What more could you ask for?"

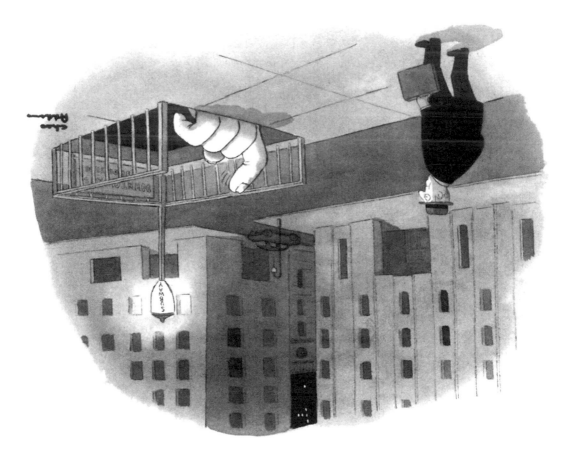

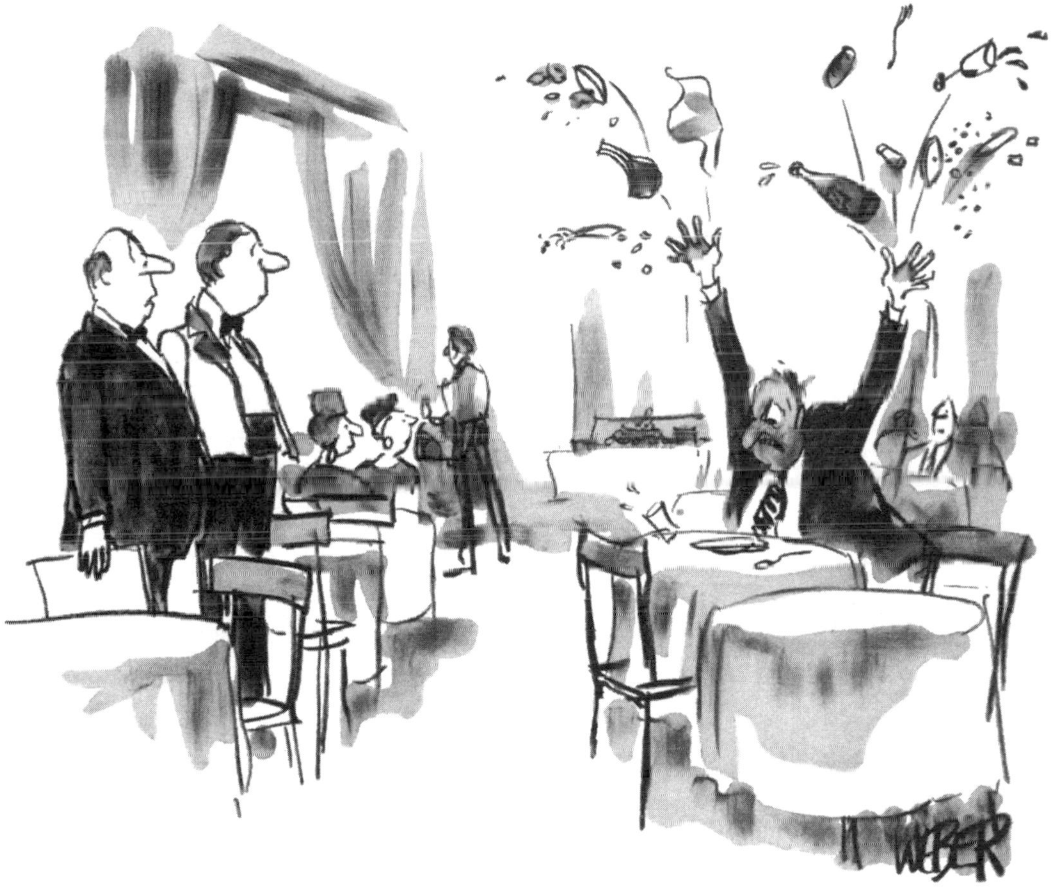
WEBER

"We can only hope he's not the Times' new food man."

THE REJECTS
I ♠ NY
I ♦ NY
I ♣ NY
R. Chast

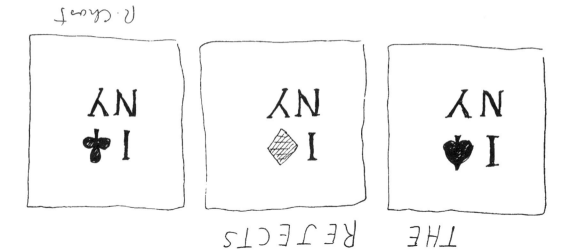

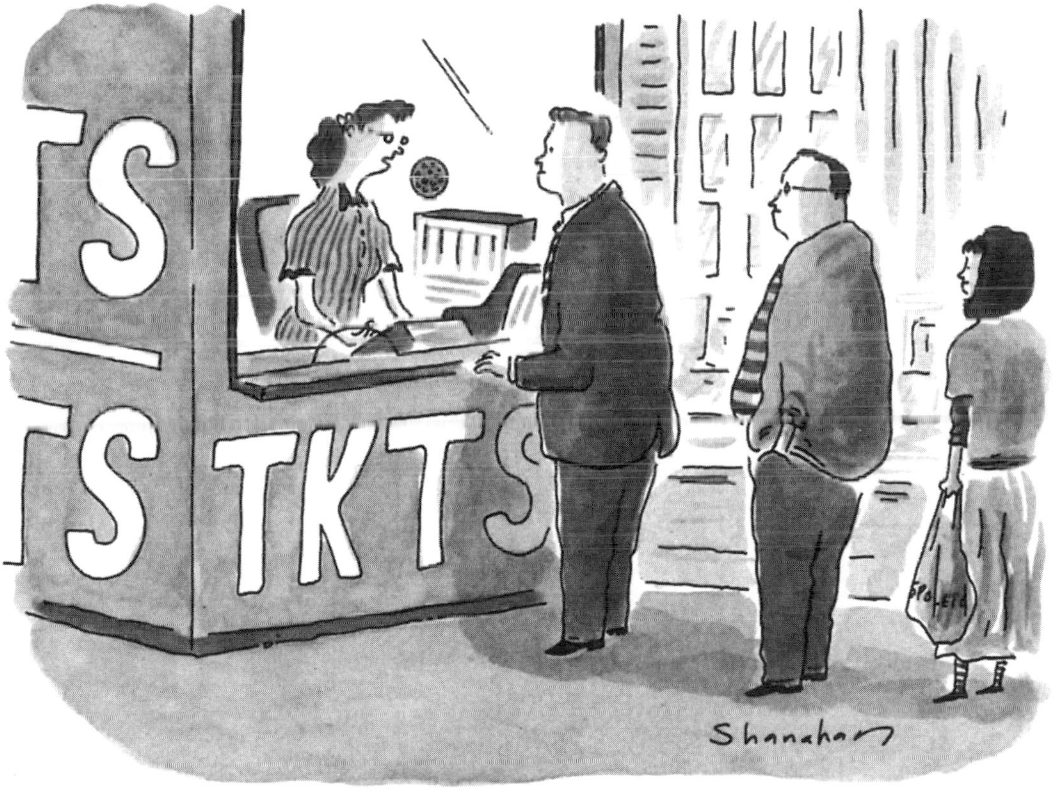
TKTS
Shanahan

"NTHNG FR 'LS MSRBLS' OR 'PHNTM.' HOW BT 'A CHRS LN'?"

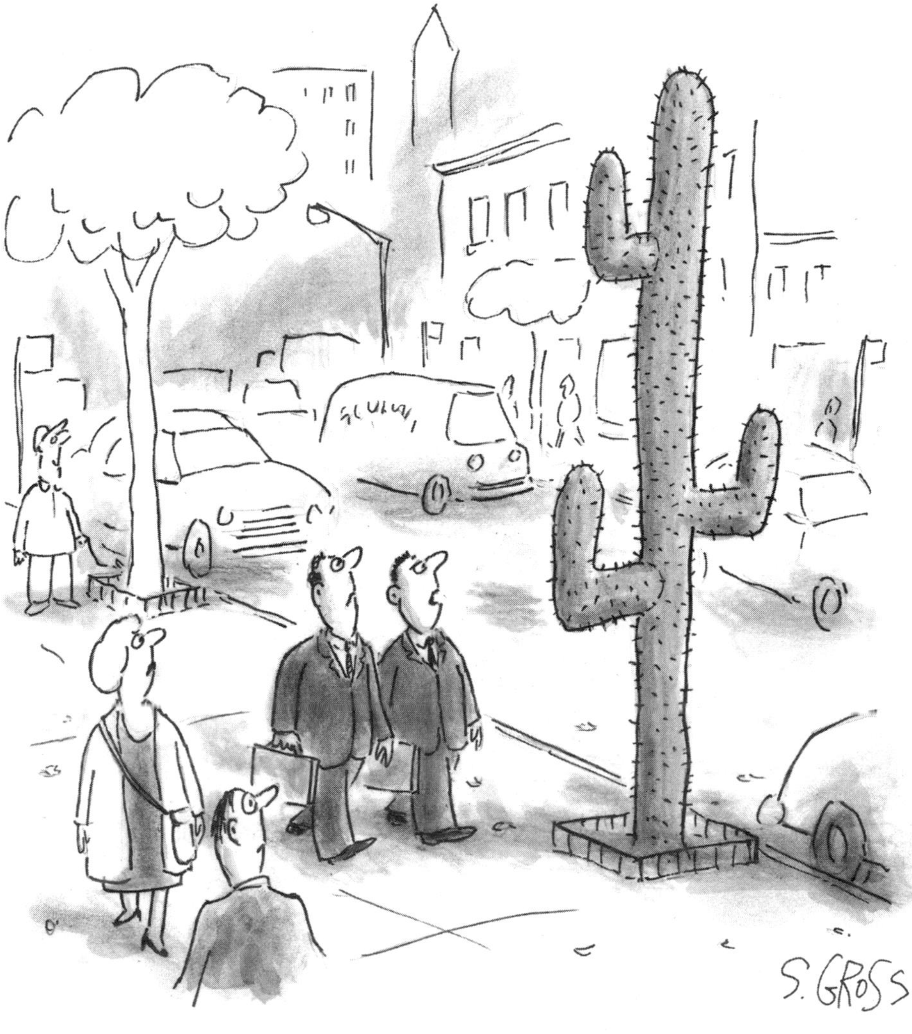
S. GROSS

"I'm starting to get concerned about global warming."

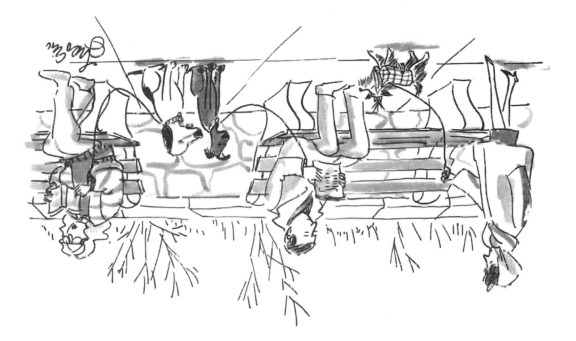

"Here comes God's gift to Central Park West."

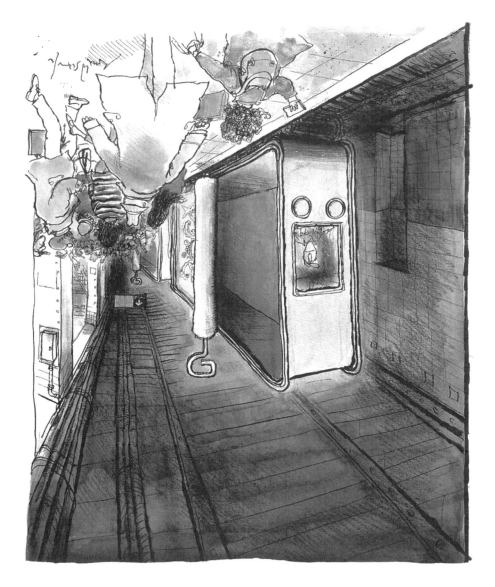

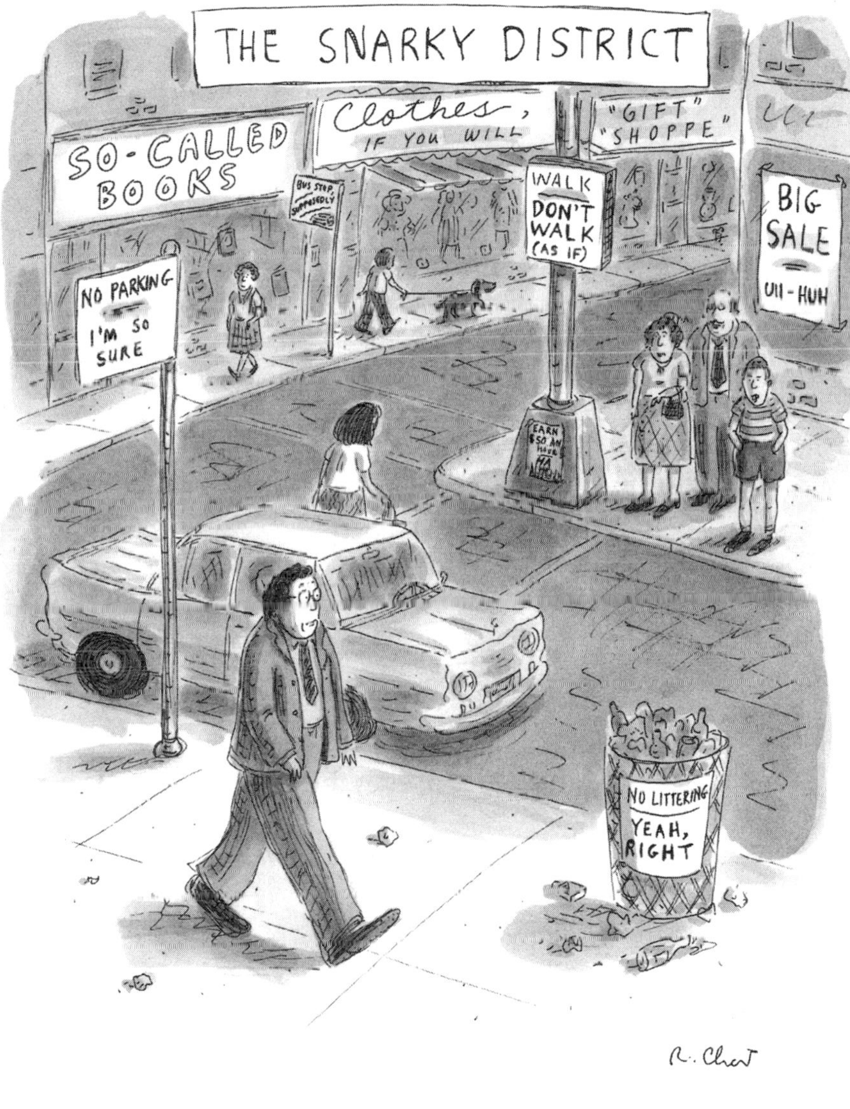
THE SNARKY DISTRICT
SO-CALLED BOOKS
BUS STOP, SUPPOSEDLY
Clothes, IF YOU WILL
"GIFT" "SHOPPE"
WALK
DON'T WALK (AS IF)
BIG SALE
UH-HUH
NO PARKING
I'M SO SURE
NO LITTERING
YEAH, RIGHT
R. Chast

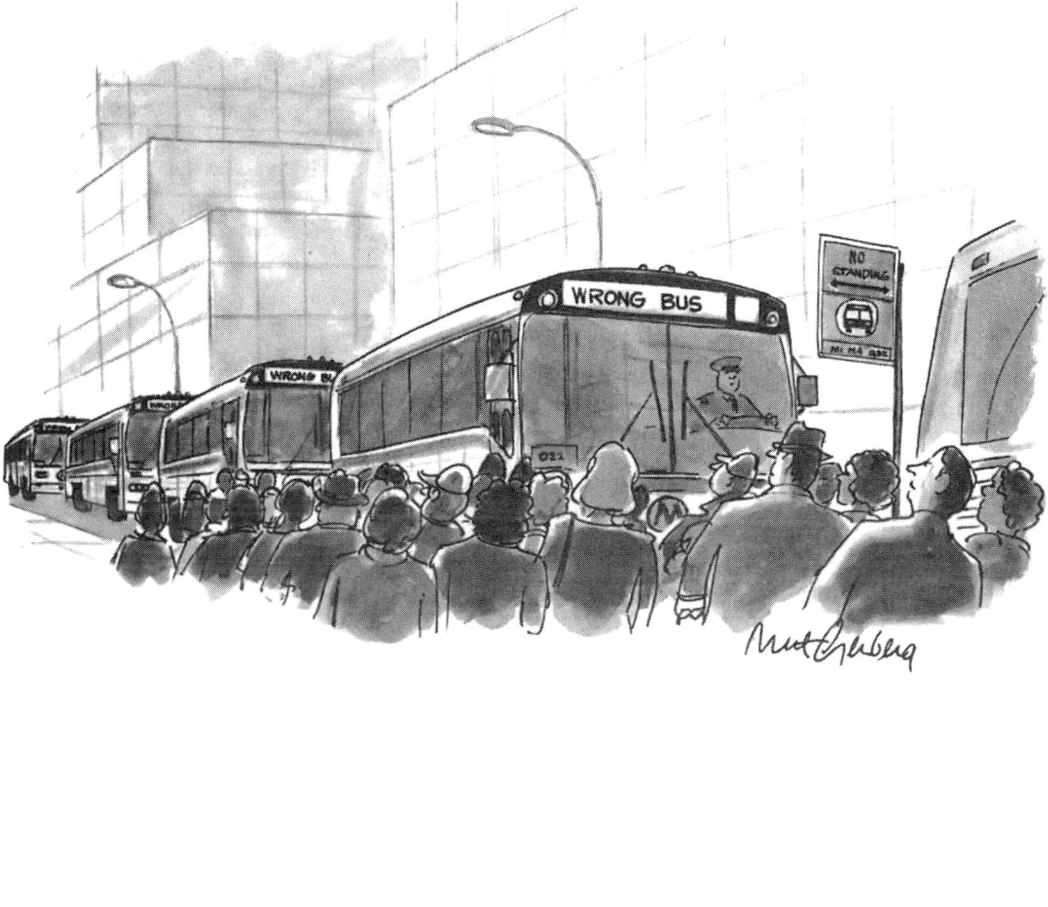
WRONG BUS
WRONG BU
NO STANDING

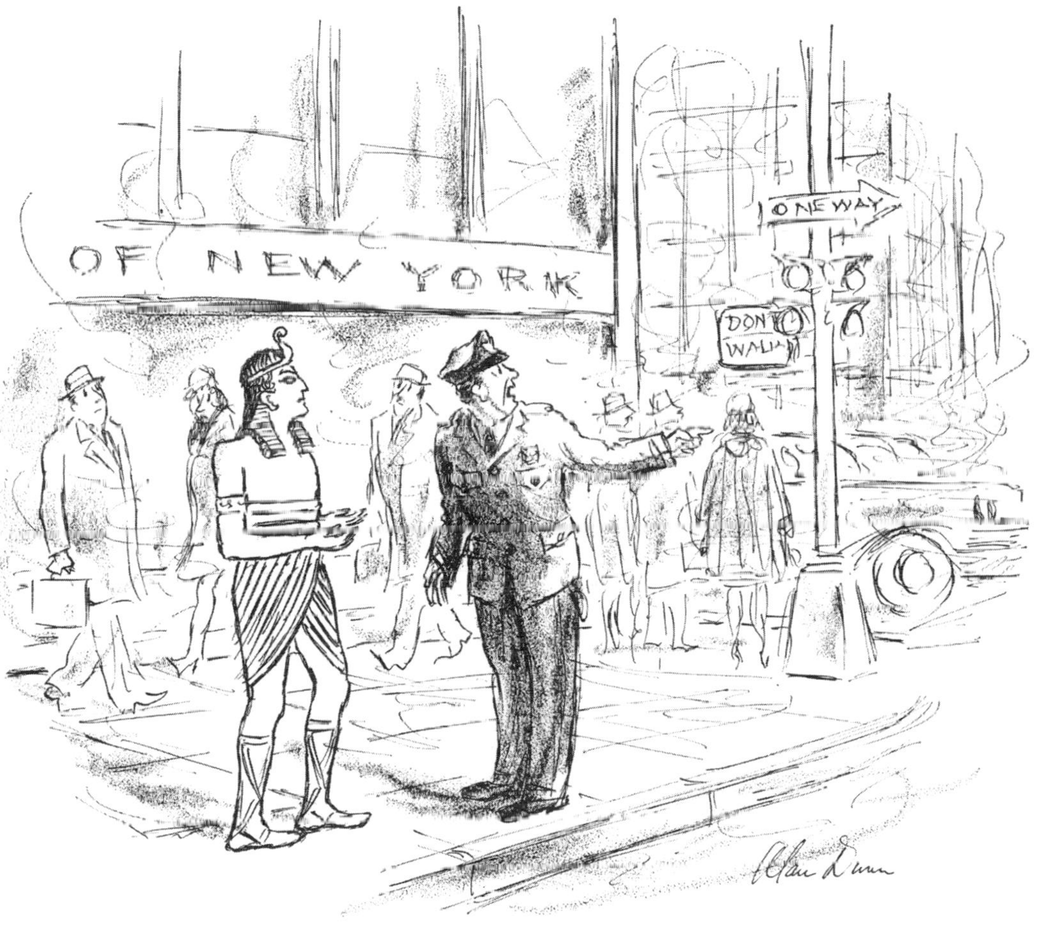
OF NEW YORK
ONE WAY
DON'T WALK

"You can't miss it. A big heap of stones, Eightieth Street and Fifth Avenue, just south of the Museum."

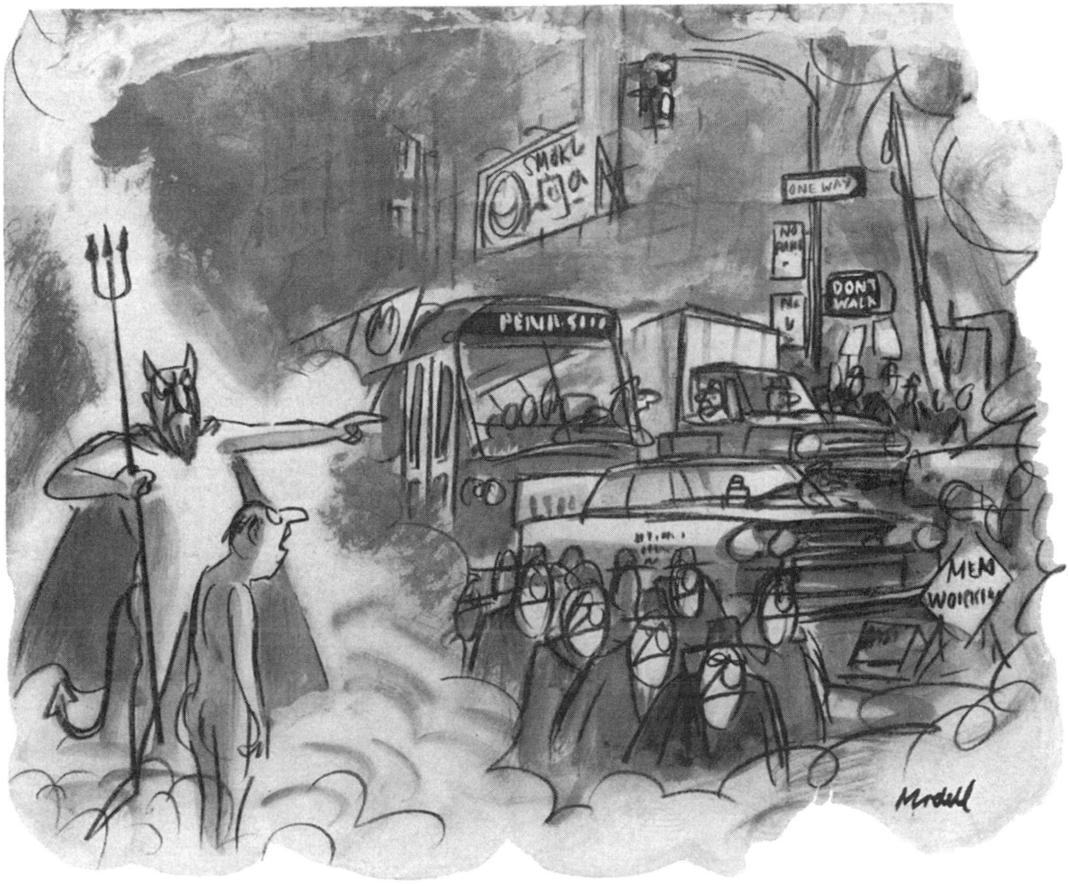
ONE WAY
DONT WALK
MEN WORKING

"Oh, no! You mean <u>this</u> is it?"

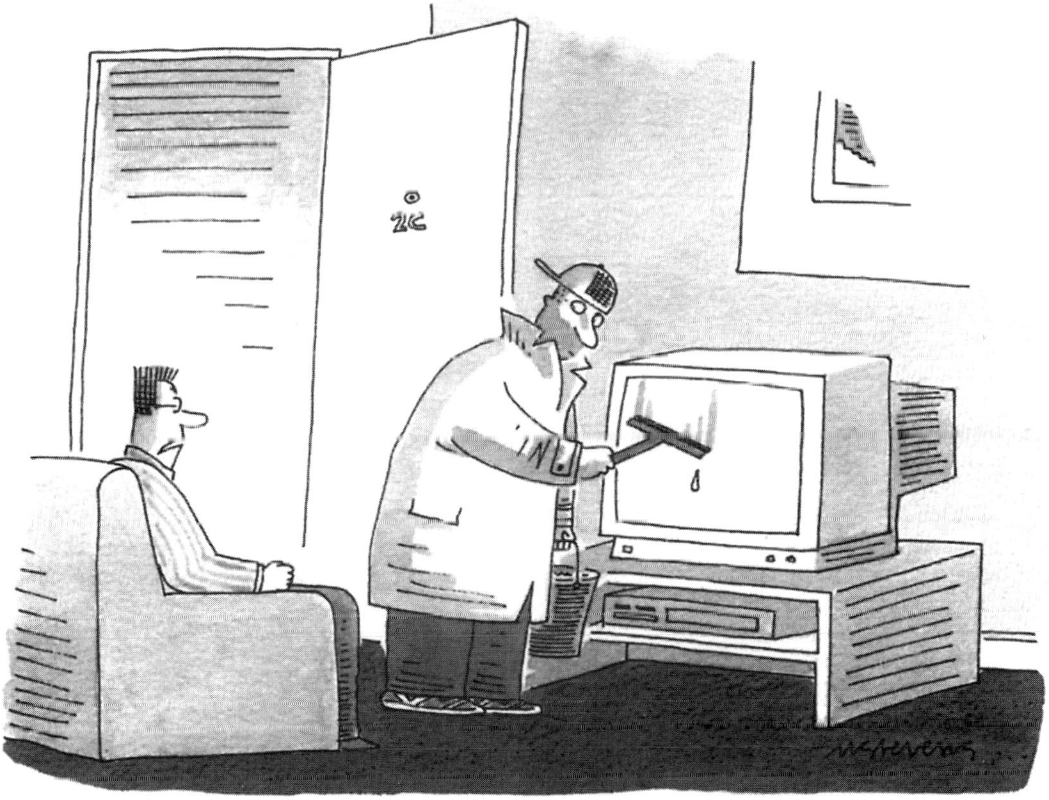
2C

"Just a damned minute!"

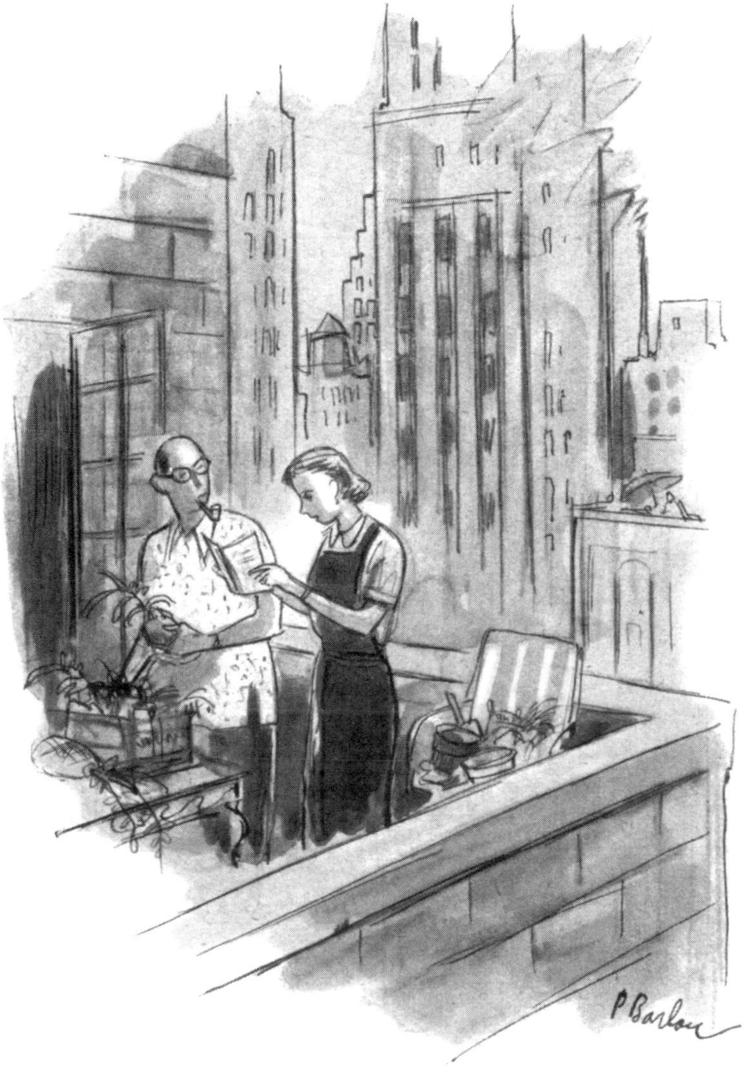
P Barlow

"Enrich the soil with humus, which can be obtained from any nearby bog..."

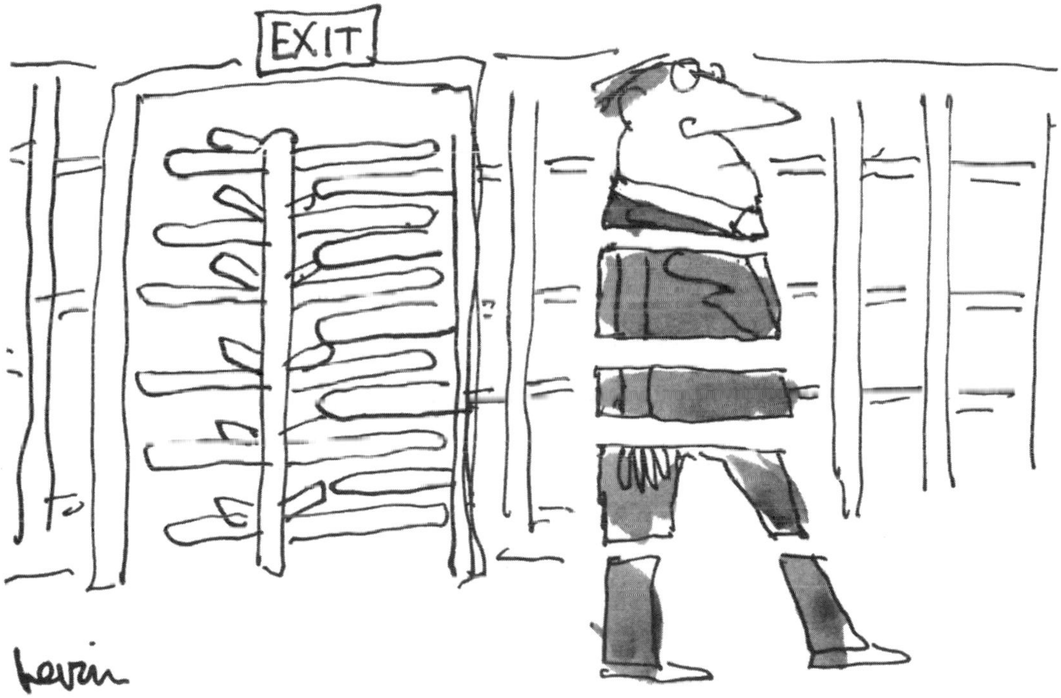
EXIT
Levin

MIRACLES ON 34th STREET
Taxi and bus did not collide.
Pay phone worked.
Vender made change without person having to buy something.
Wow! Thanks!
Saw somebody actually put trash into a receptacle.
R. Chast

EXTREME
PARKING
Rini

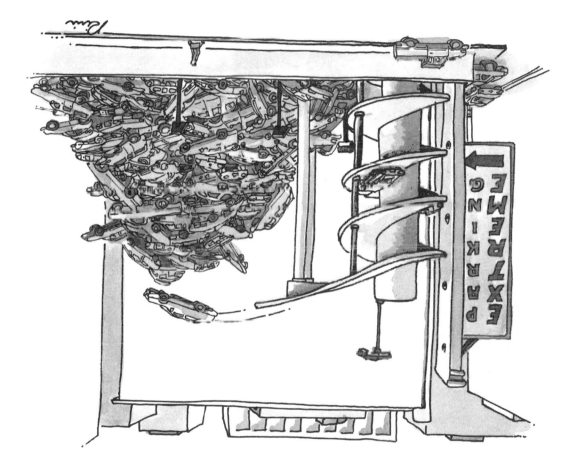

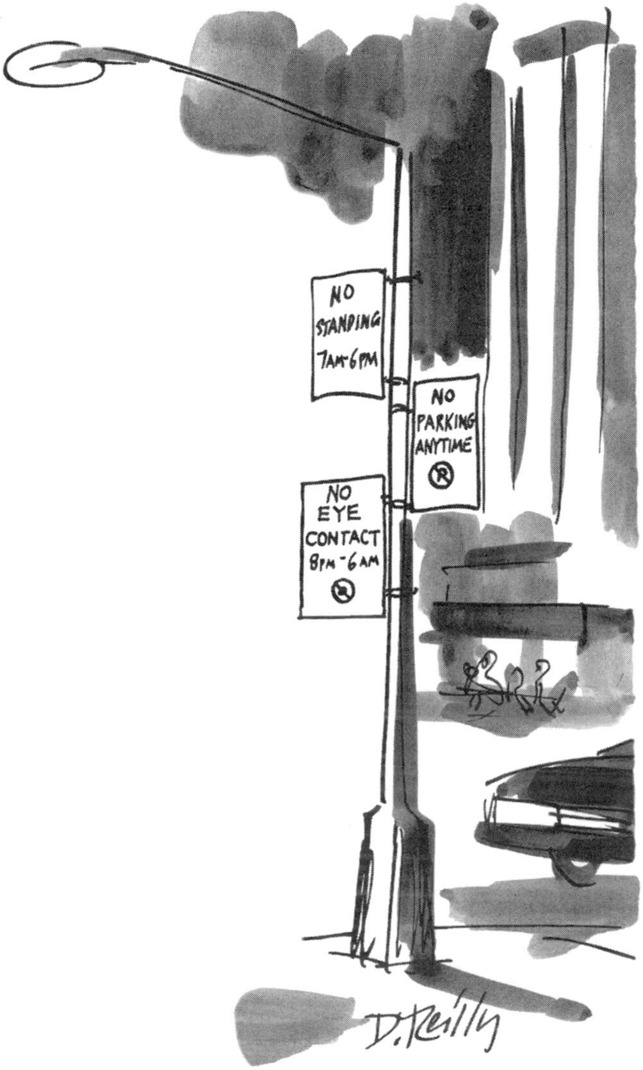
NO STANDING 7AM-6PM
NO PARKING ANYTIME
NO EYE CONTACT 8PM-6AM
D. Reilly

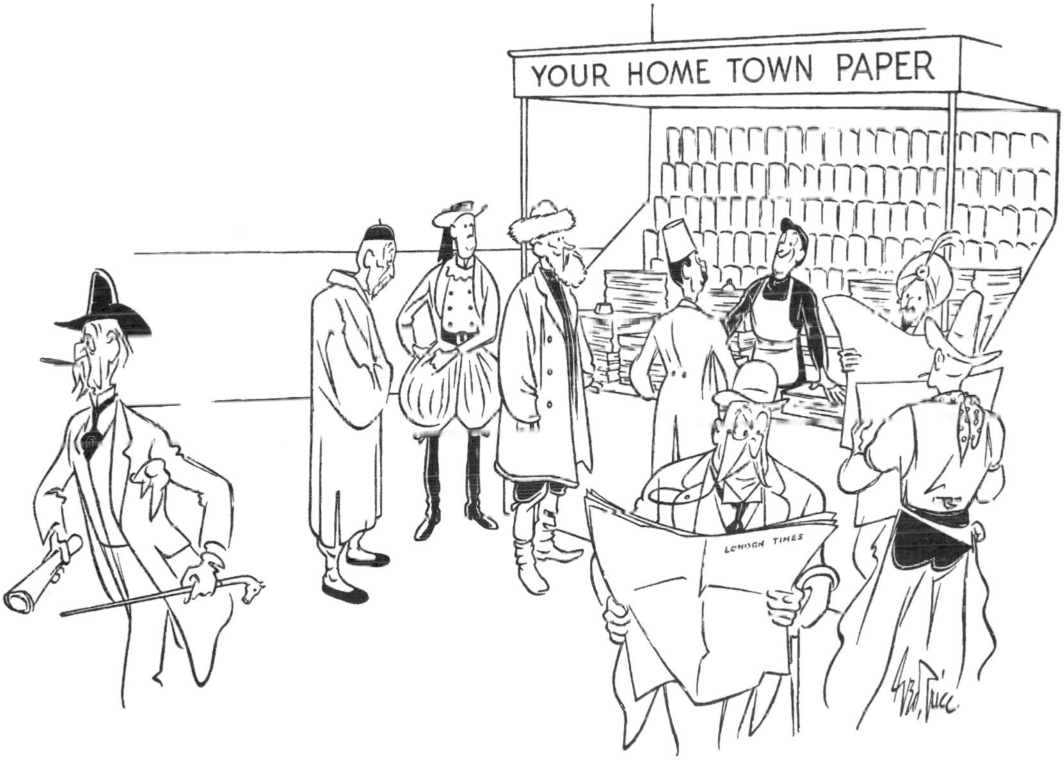
YOUR HOME TOWN PAPER
LONDON TIMES

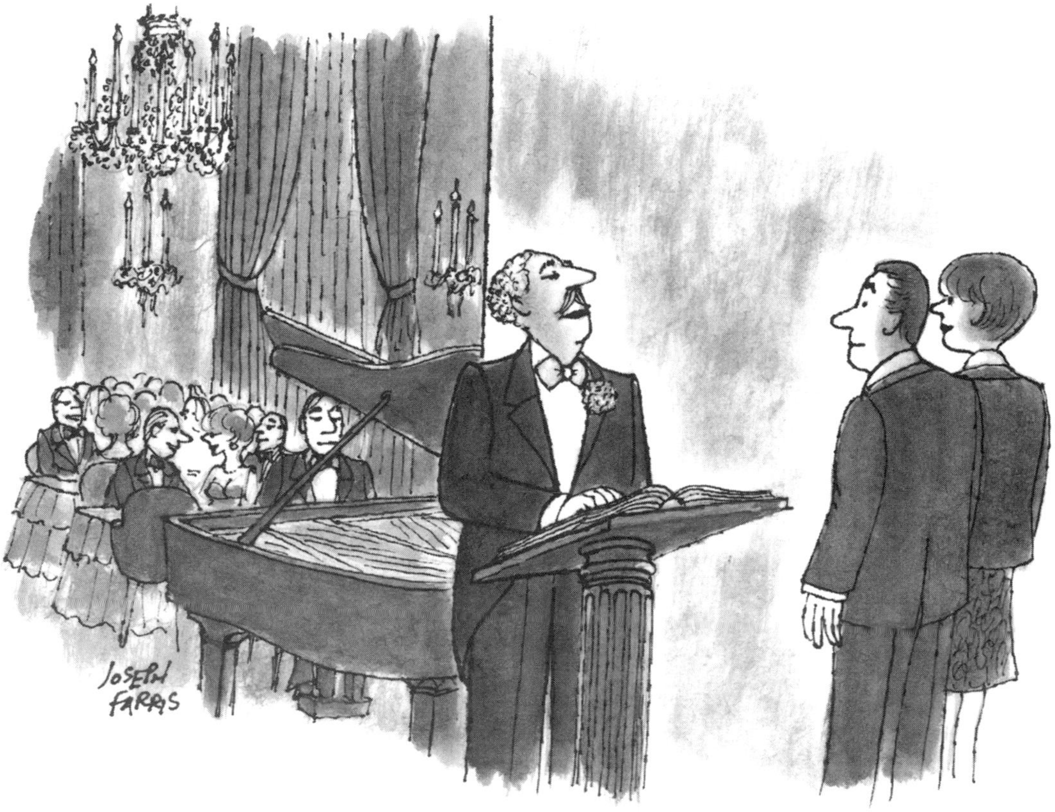
JOSEPH FARRIS

"Mets or Yankees?"

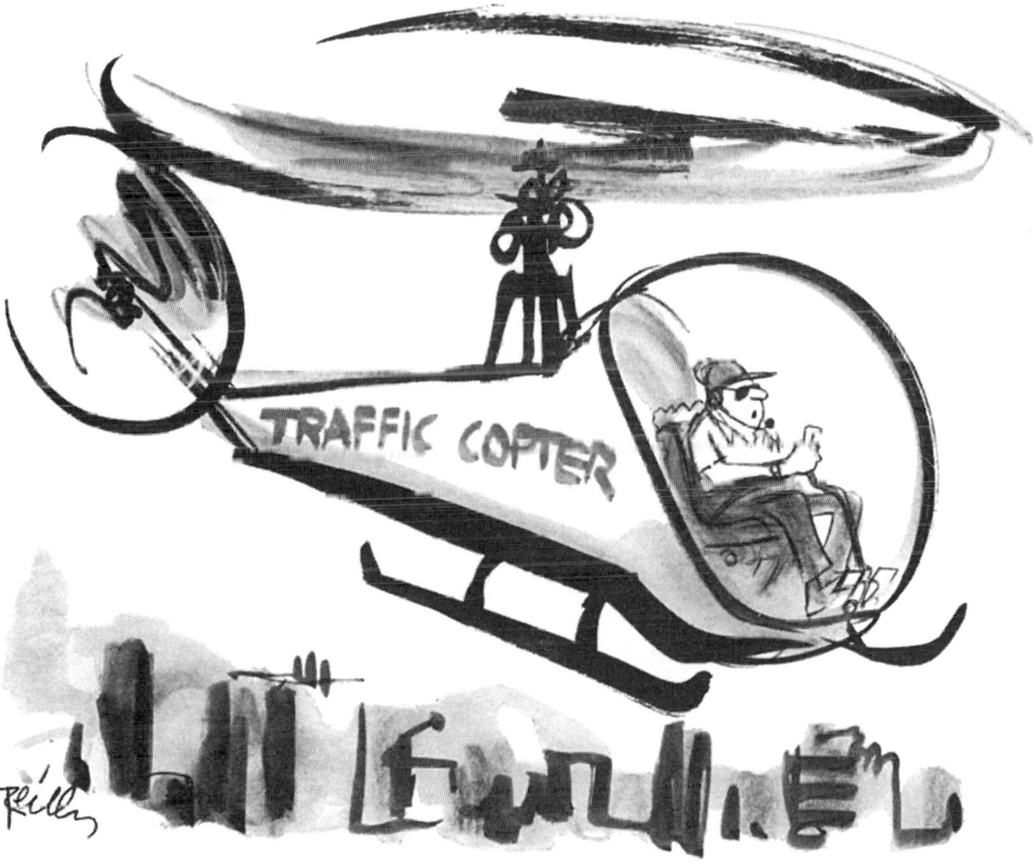
TRAFFIC COPTER
D. Reilly

"Manhattan motorists are advised to avoid the West Forties, because of a rain of fire and brimstone taking place in that area."

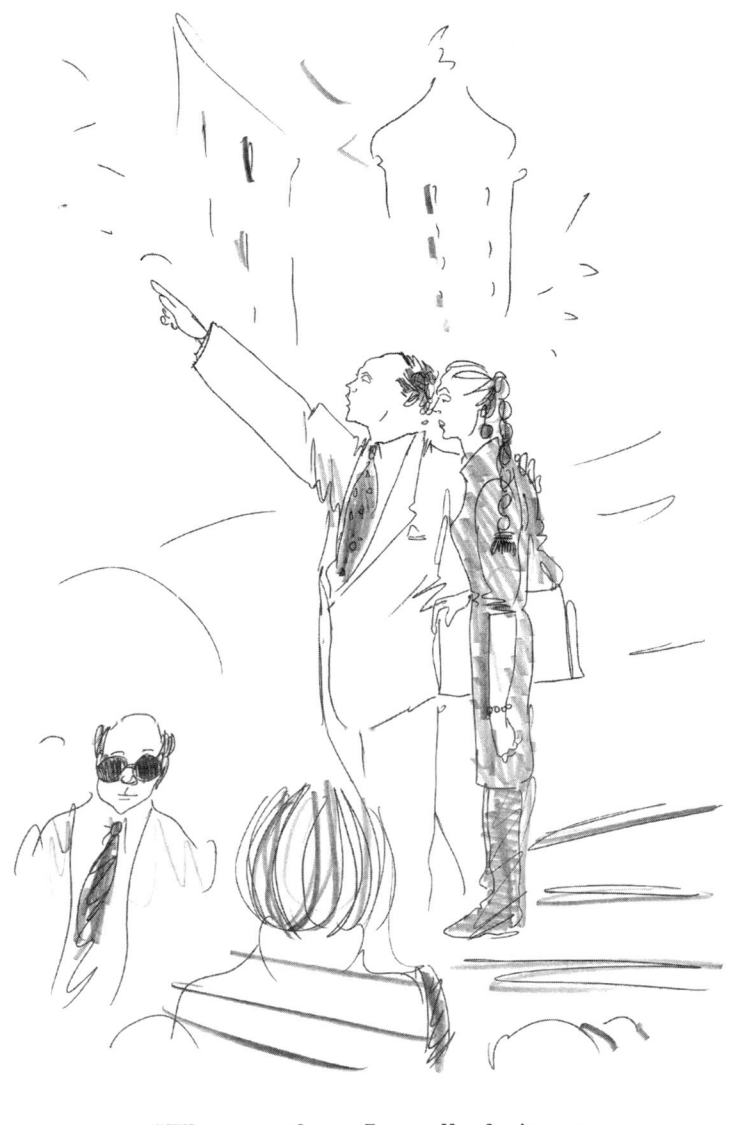

"That was fun—I usually don't go to
the Upper East Side for fun."

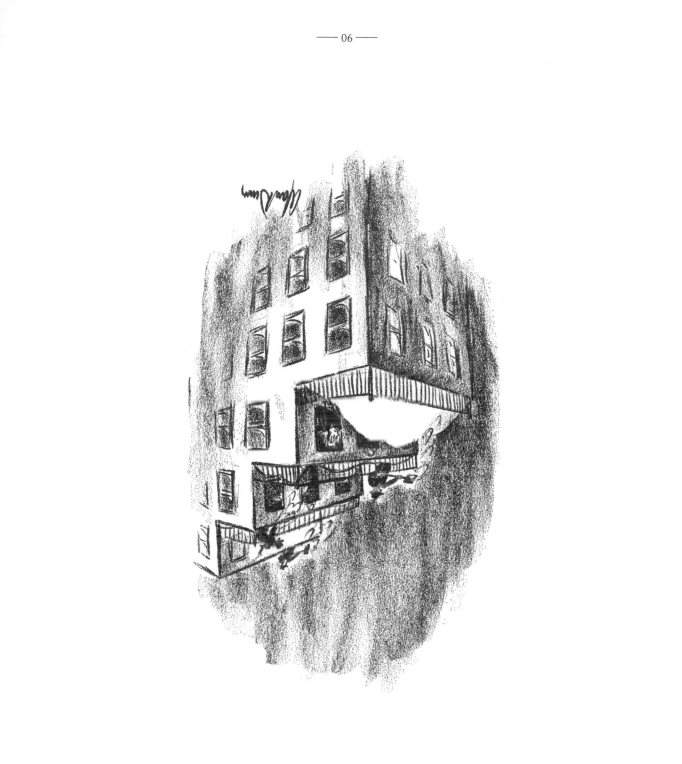

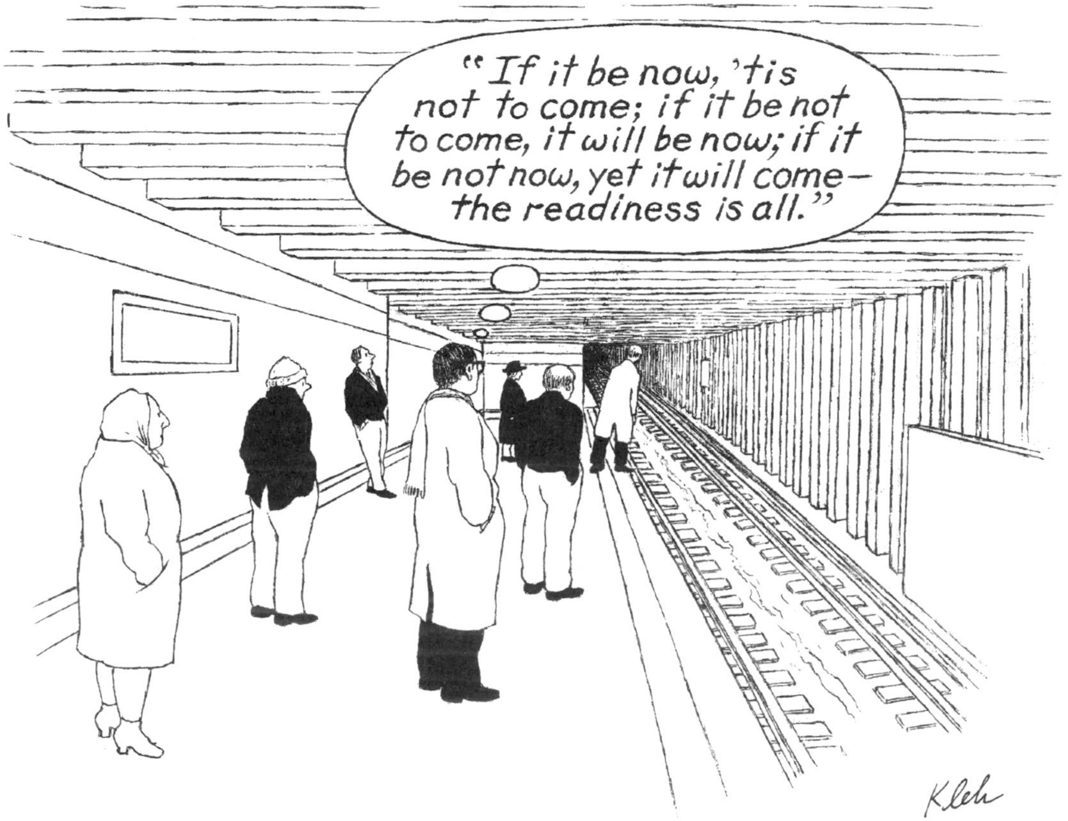
"If it be now, 'tis not to come; if it be not to come, it will be now; if it be not now, yet it will come— the readiness is all."
Kleh

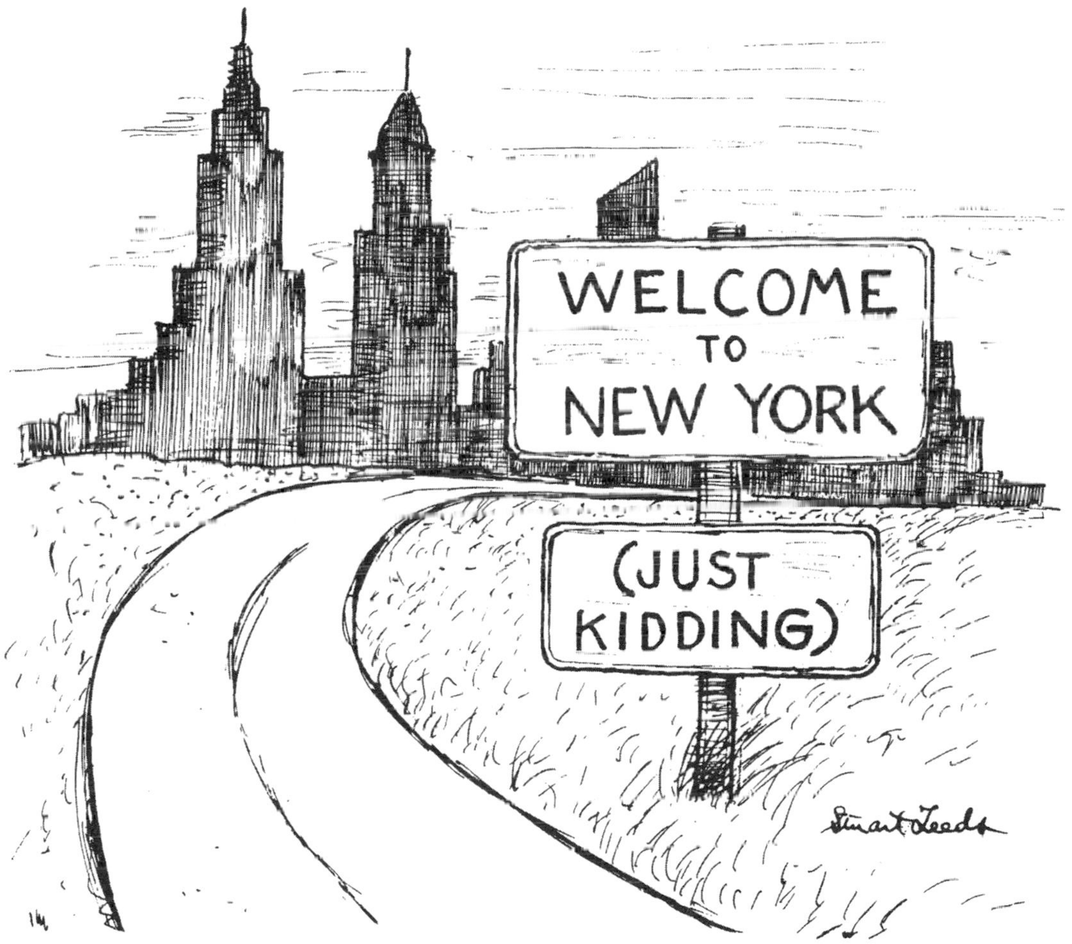
WELCOME
TO
NEW YORK
(JUST
KIDDING)
Stuart Leeds

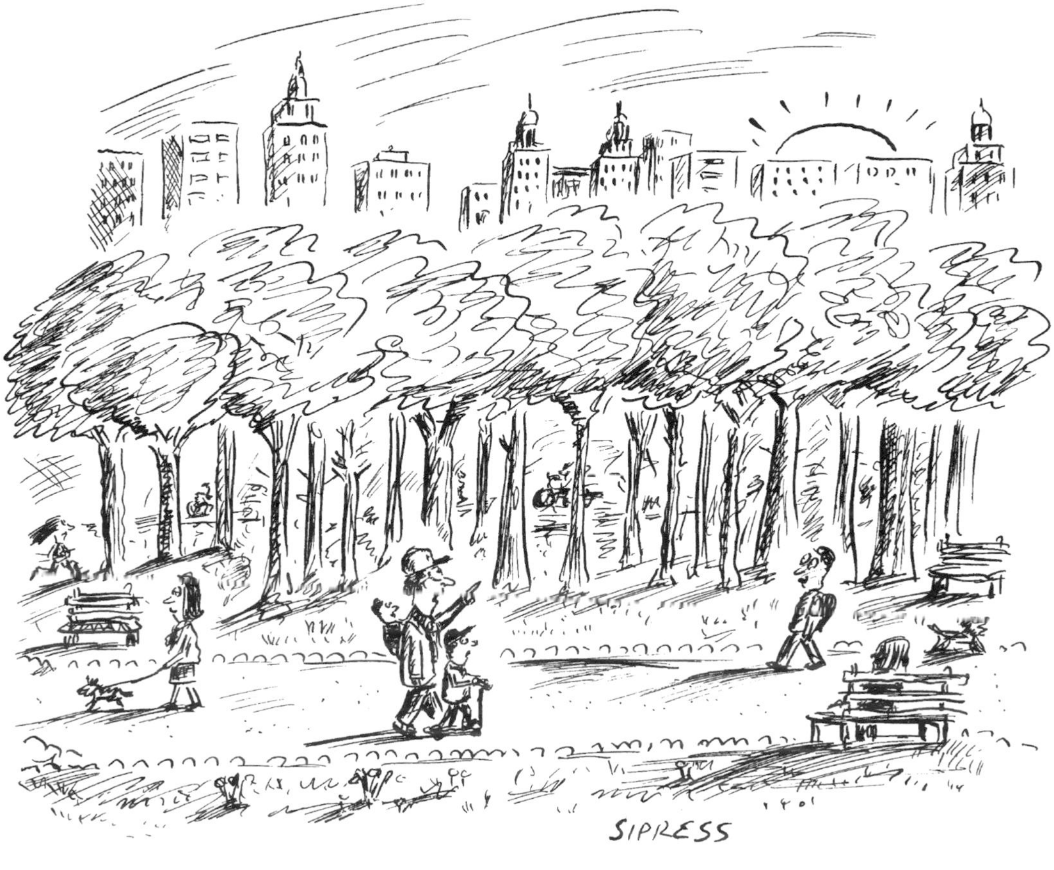
SIPRESS

"The sun rises on the Upper East Side and sets on the Upper West Side."

"There I was, the snow up to my knees and still falling steadily,
and three more blocks to the Eighty-sixth Street subway station."

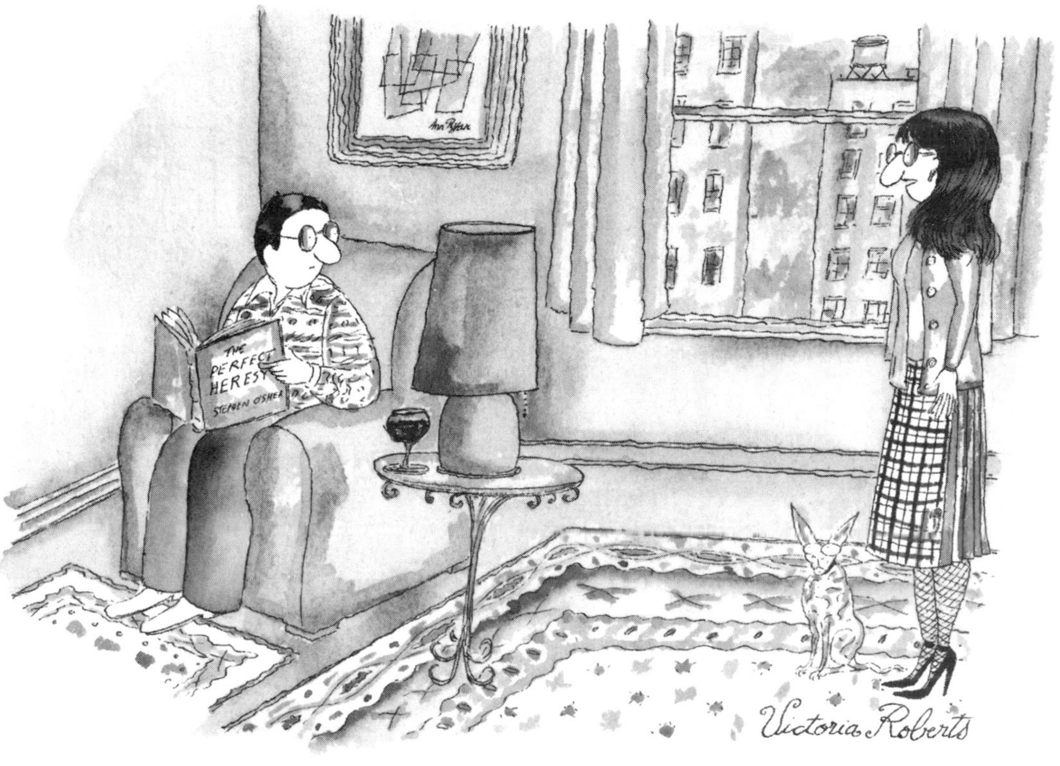
THE
PERFECT
HERESY
STEPHEN O'SHEA
Victoria Roberts

"We could move to Brooklyn, or we could live in a tent."

HAUNTED NEW YORK
The Ghost Bus of 72nd Street
Goes back and forth but never, ever stops.
BUS STOP
NO PASSENGERS
The Poltergeist of Bergdorf Goodman
Could there be any other explanation for why anyone would buy such a hideous garment?
It's You!
Totally!
The Accursed Storefront
One month, it's a gourmet cheese shop... then it's a karate studio... then a Czech restaurant... who will try their luck next?
Li'l Tikes KIDS' CLOTHES
The Ectoplasmic Super
People swear that they have seen him—but there is never any proof.
I heard he was in 6-H last week!
R. Chast

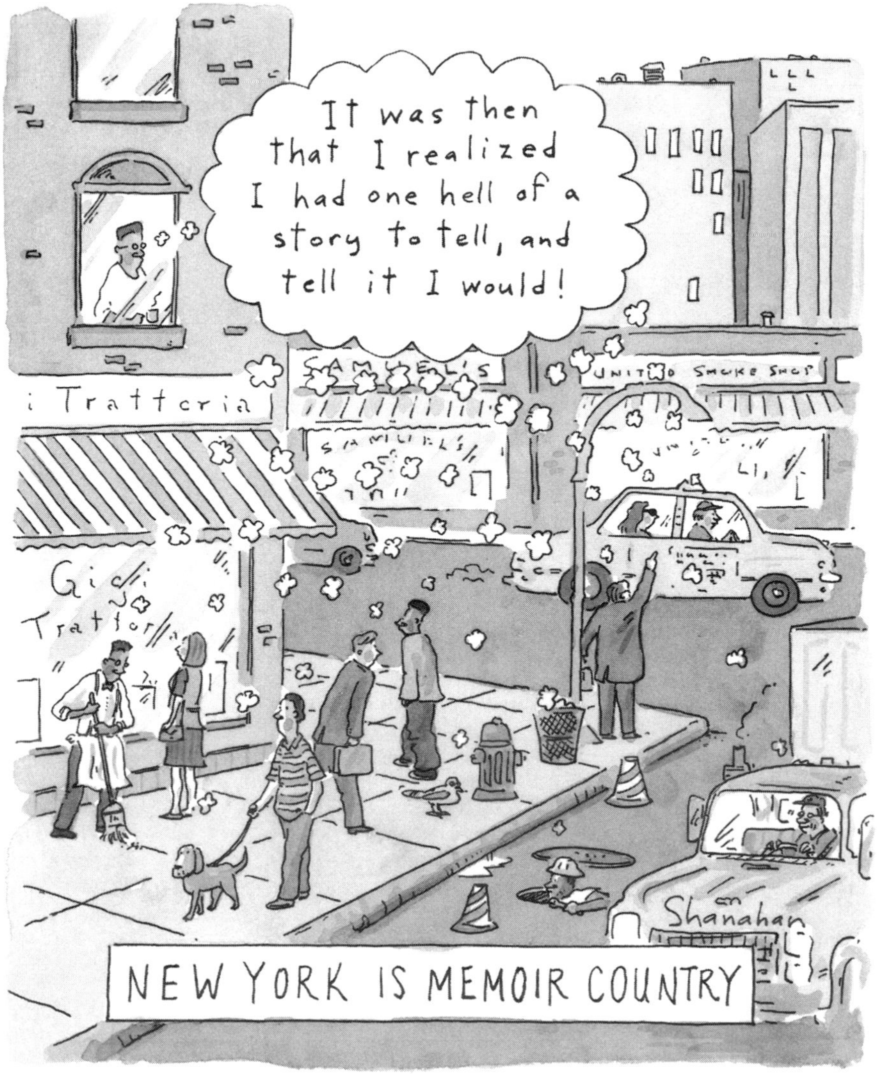
It was then that I realized I had one hell of a story to tell, and tell it I would!
i Trattoria
Gigi Trattoria
UNITED SMOKE SHOP
Shanahan
NEW YORK IS MEMOIR COUNTRY

"Can't you think of anythin' else to do but criticize Queens?"

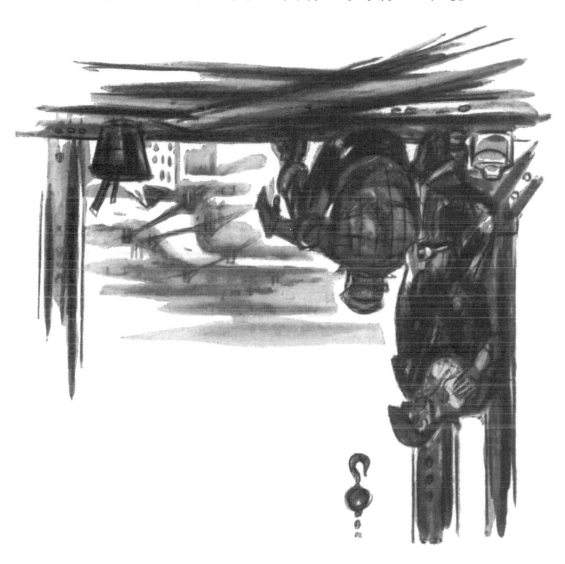

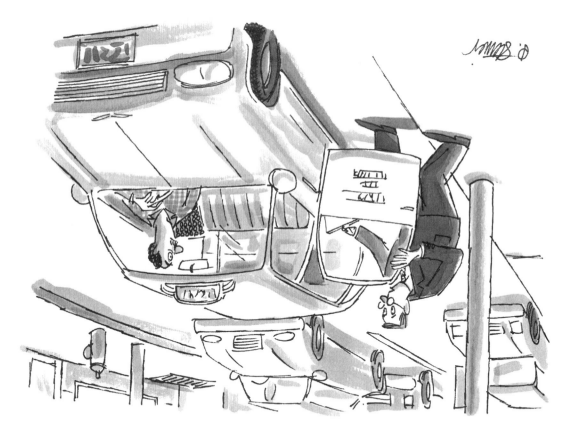

"LaGuardia, and hurry—I've got a flight in six hours."

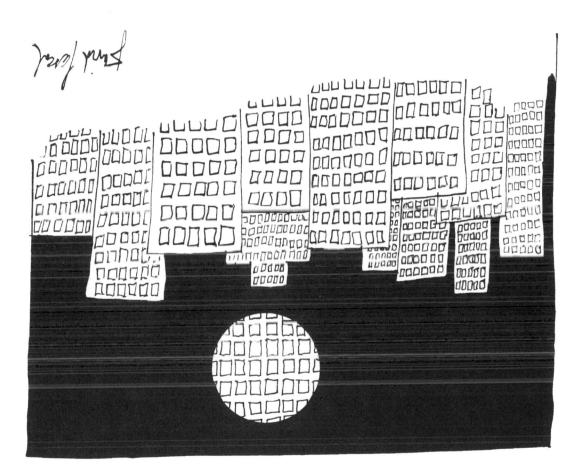

INDEX OF ARTISTS

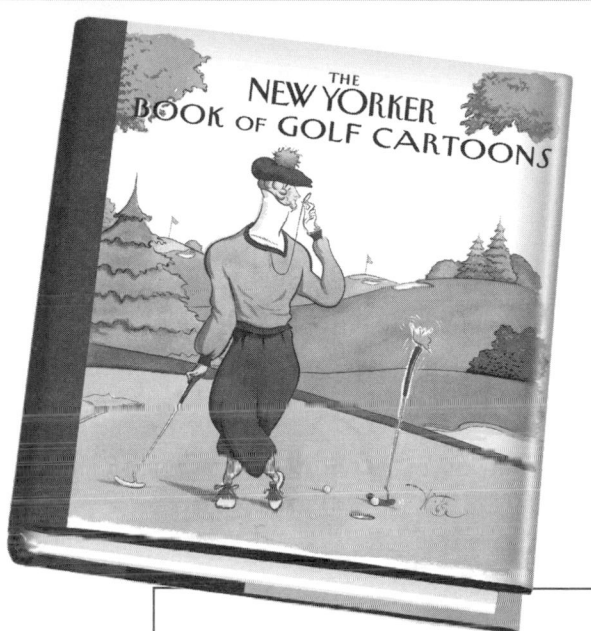
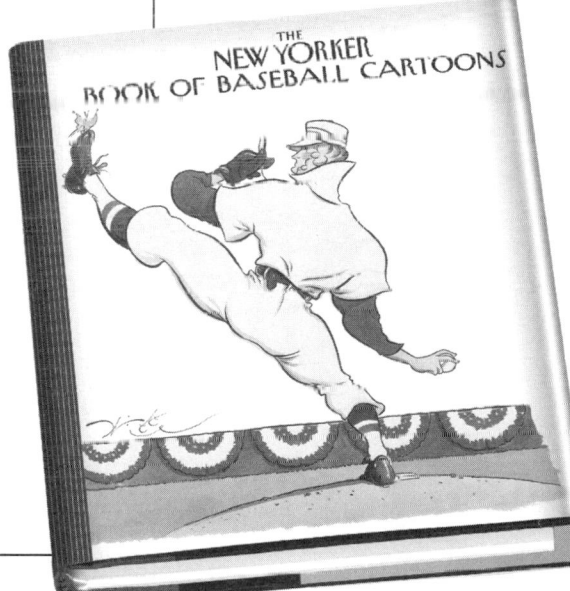
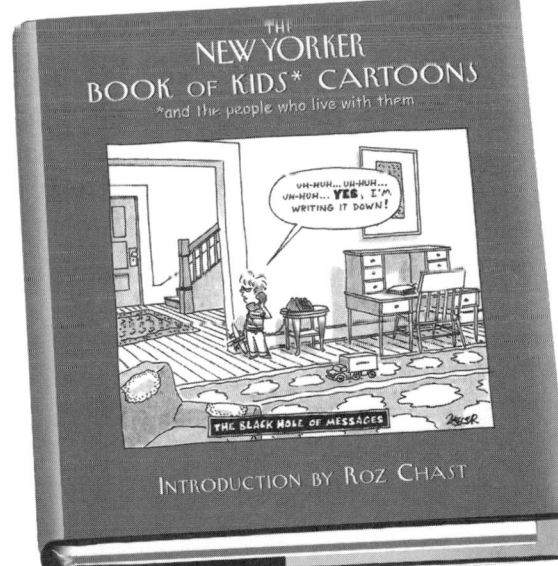

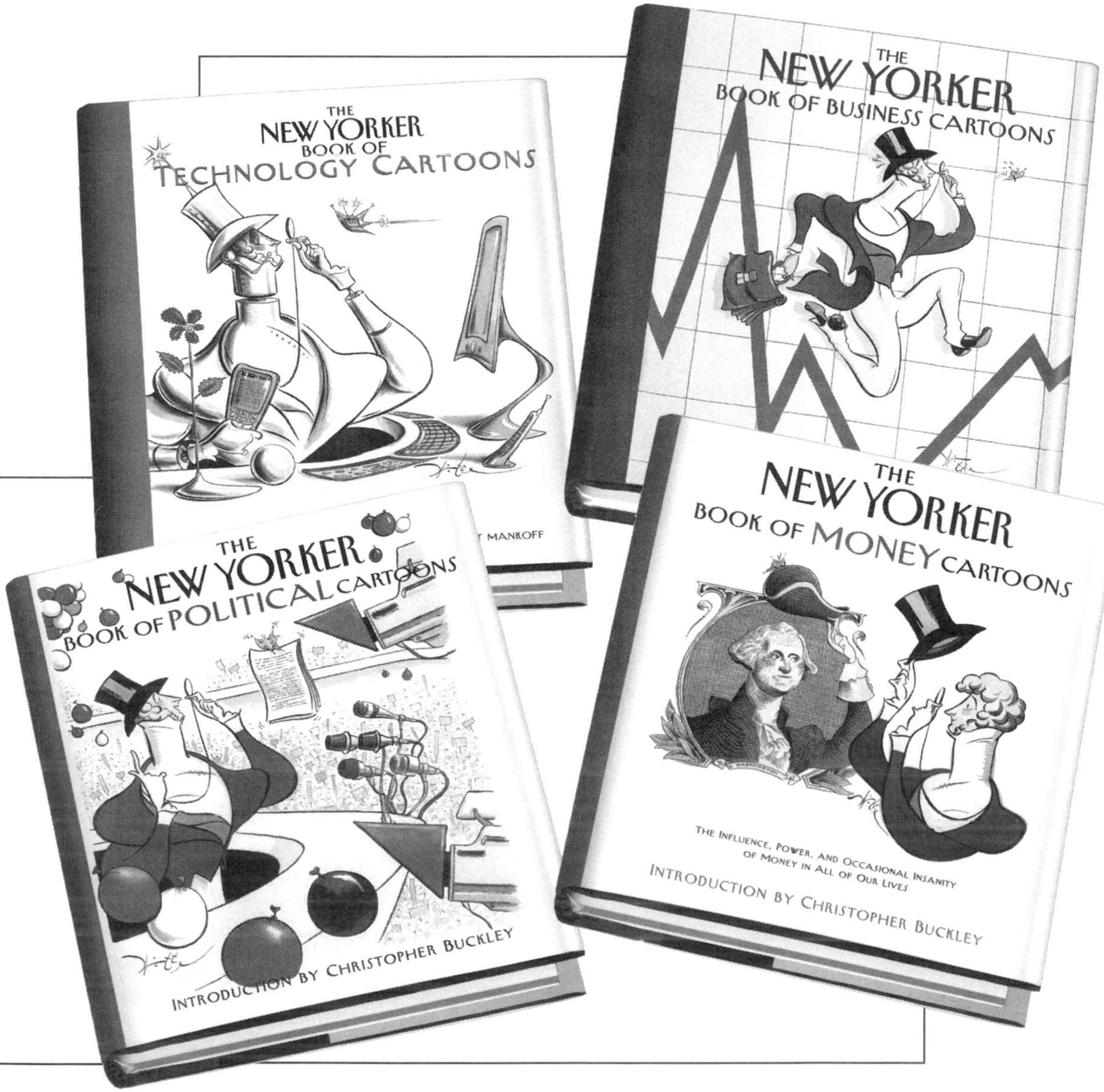
THE NEW YORKER BOOK OF TECHNOLOGY CARTOONS
MANKOFF
THE NEW YORKER BOOK OF BUSINESS CARTOONS
THE NEW YORKER BOOK OF POLITICAL CARTOONS
INTRODUCTION BY CHRISTOPHER BUCKLEY
THE NEW YORKER BOOK OF MONEY CARTOONS
THE INFLUENCE, POWER, AND OCCASIONAL INSANITY OF MONEY IN ALL OF OUR LIVES
INTRODUCTION BY CHRISTOPHER BUCKLEY

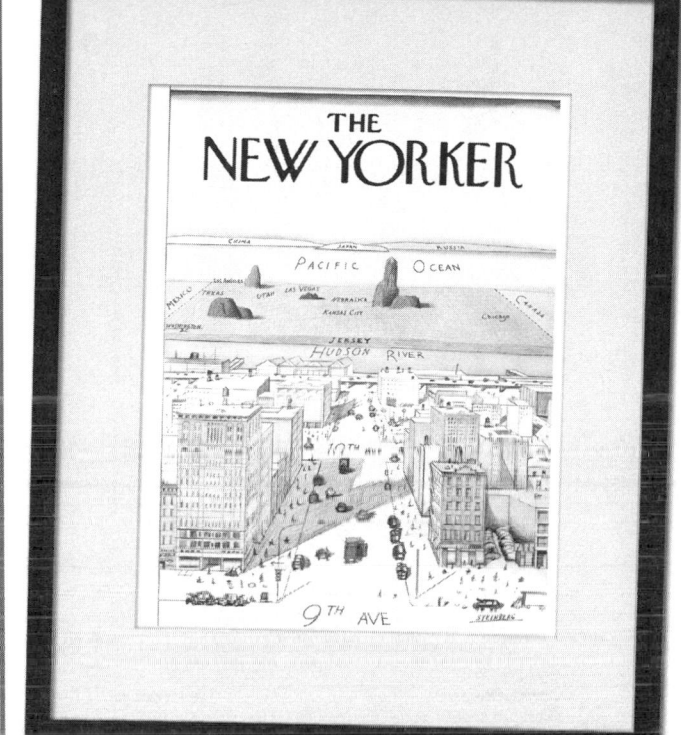
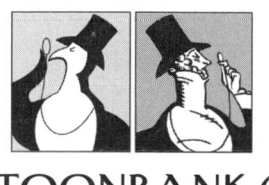
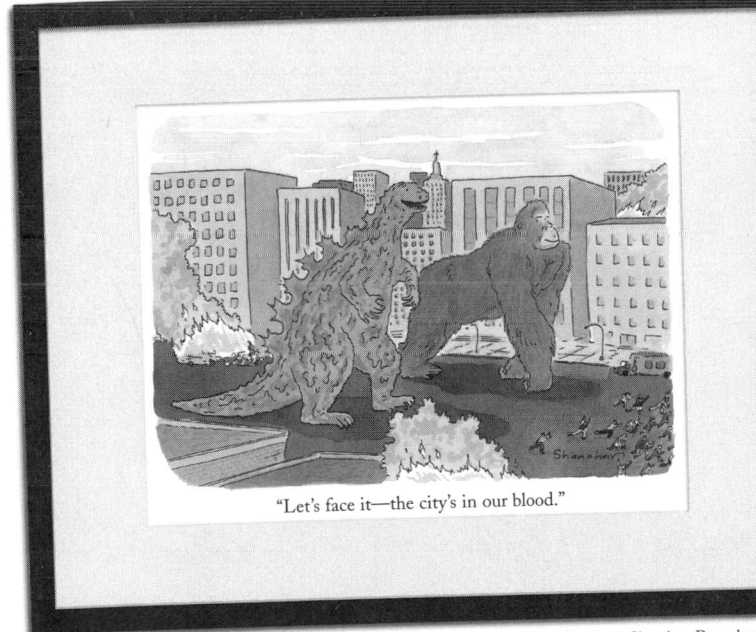

W9-AHA-119